THE CHURCH IN ACTION

THE CHURCH IN ACTION

Lectures delivered in the Divinity School of
The University of Cambridge in 1913

BY THE REV.

J. E. WATTS-DITCHFIELD, M.A

Author of "Here and Hereafter," "Fishers of Men," etc.

WITH INTRODUCTION BY THE REV.

S. A. DONALDSON, D.D

Vice-Chancellor of the University of Cambridge
Master of Magdalene

"Let us pray for the whole state of Christ's
Church Militant here on earth."

LONDON: ROBERT SCOTT
ROXBURGHE HOUSE
PATERNOSTER ROW, E.C

1913

TO MY COMRADES IN THE FIGHT.

To my Curates past and present, men of prayer and men of action, men whose life and work for Christ and His Church have been an inspiration to me.

To the noble band of women, the value of whose services for God cannot be estimated except by Him.

To these, men and women, whose work for the Church is bearing fruit in many hearts and lives, this book is dedicated as some slight appreciation of uncountable acts of loving service so freely rendered to the Author.

INTRODUCTION

I COMMEND this volume with the utmost heartiness and goodwill to all readers. The Lectures were delivered last Lent Term in the Divinity Schools, Cambridge, by the Lecturer in Pastoral Theology for the year 1913, to a large audience of Undergraduates, whom he attracted and retained from first to last: and small wonder: for the Lectures were not only full of deep spirituality and true earnestness, but were also eminently practical, sane, wide-minded, enriched with apt illustrations and humorous anecdotes.

I commend them therefore in their published form:

First, To those who heard them: they will be glad to be reminded of many a vigorous home thrust as well as of valuable advice.

Second, To Ordinands in general who will find here lessons and counsel drawn from a long experience of Parish Work singularly blessed by God.

Third, To a wider Public, men and women of whatever denomination or Religious Belief, who cannot fail to be at once benefited and entertained by the perusal of these pages.

Adsit Deus ipse hujusmodi operibus.

S. A. DONALDSON,
(*Vice-Chancellor*).

MAGDALENE COLLEGE LODGE,
CAMBRIDGE,
September 14, 1913.

CONTENTS

LECTURE THE FIRST

LECTURE THE SECOND

CONTENTS

LECTURE THE FIFTH

THE CHURCH IN ACTION

LECTURE THE FIRST

In Its Ministry

EVERY Christian is a member of the Church Militant. There is no other Church on earth, for the Church of God on earth is the fighting army of the Lord. She is the Church Militant! The Church in Action! She must be Militant or die. She must be fighting or belie her Lord. She must be the Church at war or leave unfulfilled her task of conquering the world for Christ. Her spirit must be that of aggression and never that of mere defence. Her Lord says, " Go," and go the Church must—in spite of principalities and powers, both of earth and air, she must ever march on and on, until she can lay the whole world as a trophy of victory at the feet of her Lord and King. But in this campaign her Ministers, as her officers, must lead, and so in the course of study upon which we are entering this evening, our first consideration must be concerning the Ministry of the Church—the call to this ministry, its work, its sphere, its equipment.

I. **The Call to the Ministry.**

(a) *By the Voice of God*. Not every Christian man is called to the Ministry. No one would deny that men are called to the work of teaching or to the work of healing.

But Christian men are also called to the colliery, the factory, the shop, the bank, and the bar, and in fact to every honourable work. It may safely be said that not more than one man in five hundred is called to the special work of the Ministry ; and if that be so, every Christian layman, before he takes Holy Orders, must be satisfied that he is the one so called, and not merely one of the other four hundred and ninety-nine, whose witness for Christ is required in the ordinary walks of life. Various reasons are advanced by men for seeking Holy Orders. The man who craves the highest duties from the lowest of motives, the man who thinks of little but to better his own position may be dismissed with contempt. Others, it is possible, seek admission into the Ministry because they wish to devote all their time to the work of God, and because they think they see in it a wider sphere of usefulness. But they are not necessarily called. We may applaud the motive but doubt the reality of the call. Others point to the work which they have been able to do for God as lay-men, and suggest that the fact that God has given them such success constitutes a call to ministerial work, forgetting that the very reverse may be the case, and that God in honouring it, may have but set His seal to their life of work as a Layman. " No man taketh this honour unto himself " but he that is called of God, and a candidate for Holy Orders is compelled to face the question, " Do you trust that you are inwardly moved by the Holy Ghost to take upon you this Office ? "

God moves men in various ways. He moves some as distinctly as He moved the prophet Amos, who said as he looked back upon his life, " The Lord took me as I followed the flock and said, 'Go prophesy.'" He moves others towards their life-work as gradually and as quietly as the night passes into day. But whatever the method, it is certain that when a man is truly called, the Holy Spirit will in some manner convey the will of God to his heart, so that one so chosen will feel something of that which caused St. Paul to cry out " Woe is me if I preach not the Gospel." The man who is " called " may be sure that in some way he will know that he is called. Our blessed Master said, " As Thou hast sent Me into the world, even so have I also sent them into the world," and as the Dove lighted upon Him and the Voice of God sounded in His ear, so the Holy Ghost falls upon the man whom the Lord has chosen, and gives to him the ear to hear the command, " Go, this day have I chosen thee."

(b) *By the Church.*—We read in Acts xiii. 2 that God did not merely " call " Barnabas and Saul but that He revealed His choice to the Church. The Holy Spirit said, " Separate me Barnabas and Saul for the work whereunto I have called them," and they were sent forth not only by God but by the Church, as recorded in verse three. And so it has ever been; the Church and the man are both moved, the one to send and the other to go, and so commissioned by God and the Church, the man goes forth as the Minister of God to battle for his Lord.

Great as is the " High Calling " it should ever tend to a realization of one's own unworthiness, and anything savouring of pride should have no place in heart or life. Bishop Lightfoot's words may well be recalled, " Remember this commission in yourselves, but do not parade it before others. Do not vulgarize it. An assertion of authority by a young clergyman provokes only opposition. Rather approve yourselves to

your people as ambassadors of Christ by delivering the
message of Christ, by doing the work of Christ, by
living the life of Christ."

II. The Ministry of the Church of England.

It is that, to quote Archbishop Benson, of the
" Catholic, Apostolic, Reformed, Protestant " Church
of England.   " The Church of England ! "   Although
we are taught in the Bidding Prayer to pray for
" the whole congregation of Christian people dispersed
throughout the world," and although, as John Wesley
once said, "We are the friends of all and the enemies of
none," yet first and foremost we must be loyal Churchmen.   As Christians we hold in common with Roman-
ists and with Nonconformists, such doctrines as the
Trinity, the Divinity of our Lord, the Incarnation,
and the Atonement, yet at the same time we have our
own definite position, going further in many directions
than the Nonconformists and stopping short of much
that the Roman accepts.   We believe in the Holy
Catholic Church ; we are Catholics, and because we are
so truly Catholic we are also Protestants, protesting
with all our might for that which is Catholic and
Apostolic.   We are proud of our inheritance as members
of the Church of England—we value her threefold
Orders, her Creed, and her Articles, we maintain the
Faith once delivered to the Saints which she proclaims
therein ; we realize the supreme position which the
Holy Scriptures have in her teaching ; we recognize
the place which the two Sacraments occupy in the life
of her children ; we rejoice in her history, and we
thank God for her share in moulding the character of the
nation ; we praise God for her Saints—for their learning, for their piety, for their lives—and in our hearts we
realize that notwithstanding her many faults the Church

of England is, to-day, the greatest force making for righteousness in the whole world. If any of you, my brothers, do not feel thus towards the Church of England and if you cannot wholeheartedly conform to her doctrine, order, and discipline then I would urge you to go elsewhere and toil in other fields, and may the God, Who at sundry times and in divers manners spake in time past unto the fathers by the prophets " (Heb. i. 1), bless you.

III. **England requires a Ministry to Proclaim the Christ as the one Hope of the World.**

England is seething with unrest. The working classes have awakened to their condition and also to their power. Fifty years ago they were largely asleep. Education was defective and the working man, generally speaking, had a narrow vision, his boundaries being the village or the town in which he lived. The world outside was almost as hazy and ethereal to him as Heaven. Now all this is altered. The school, the printing press, the cheap excursion, have contributed to open his eyes, not merely to the condition of many of his class, to their slum dwellings, to their long hours, to their sweated labour, but also to the vast wealth of the country and to its unequal distribution. It is not surprising there is unrest. But how is rest to be obtained ? Not alone through better homes, larger wages, shorter hours of labour, although these ought in the Name of Christ to be obtainable by all. If " rest " came that way, then the West End in possessing all these things which most men are seeking, would be Heaven indeed, but, alas, the West End has sorrows, disappointments, heart-aches, equal to those of the East End, for, after all, these things are part of the common lot of men. What then ? Down the ages we hear the Saviour's

Voice, " Come unto Me and I will give you rest." And all history tells us that there is none other name given among men whereby they can obtain rest, but *"The Name"* that is above every name.

IV. **The Main Work of the Ministry is to Proclaim Christ as the Saviour of men.**

" As Thou hast sent Me," said Christ, " *so* have I sent them." His purpose must be ours and can we doubt what that purpose is when we picture the scene in the Synagogue at Nazareth as He opened the Scriptures and read ?—" *He hath anointed Me* to preach the Gospel to the poor, He hath sent Me to heal the broken-hearted, to preach deliverance to the captives, and recovering of sight to the blind, to set at liberty them that are bruised, to preach the acceptable year of the Lord (St. Luke iv. 18, 19). So have I sent them." His work is also ours. He came to put an end to all sin by bringing men to God. If we are in any doubt as to the *one* work for which we are to be ordained let us ask, " What does God want more than anything else ? What does the Christ most desire ? " The Cross will give the answer to both questions—the Salvation of Men. The price paid for the souls of men reveals how dear they are to the heart of God, and so the Church sends her Ministers forth " to seek for Christ's sheep scattered abroad." As Christ Jesus came into the world to seek and to save sinners, so we enter into the Ministry to co-operate with Him in the same work. We do not become Ministers of the Word and of the Sacraments simply to attract crowds—an aeroplane can do that much better—but to seek and to save souls. Nor are we ordained Ministers of Christ simply to be the good ' bat,' the champion at golf, the wonder of the athletic world, or to be the " jolly companion," the " life " of

the Club, of the " At Home " or the " Whist Drive."
We are to seek to save souls.

With respect to what is called ' Church Work ' we
do well to remember the words of John Wesley to his
preachers, " Your business is not to preach so many
times and to take care of this or that Society, but to
save as many souls as you can." This then is *the* work
whether in the Pulpit, in administering the Sacraments,
when visiting from door to door, when attending the
Clubs, when teaching in the Sunday Schools or when
preaching in the Open Air. Wherever we are, first
and all the time our work is that of winning souls for
God. Angels only rejoice, the pierced heart of the
Christ is only made glad when the souls of men pass
from death unto life, by contact with the Crucified.
Let it ring in our ears by day and by night, " I am
sent to seek that which was lost."

V. The Sphere of the Ministry.

The late Bishop King (of Lincoln) always emphasized
the fact that men were ordained to the world and not to
any particular parish or even country. The Lord Who
sent Jonah to Nineveh and Who prevented St.Paul from
going to Bithynia, is still He Who rules His Church.
Many recognize that before a man enters the Ministry
He must hear God calling him, but how few apparently
remember that when the Ministry is entered, every
step of the Ministerial life must still be ordered by Him.
Shame on the man who looks out for the easy curacy,
the " nice parish " and for the Vicar who seems to have
influence with patrons. Verily such will have their
reward. Where does God want me ? In China or in
Whitechapel ? In South London or in that difficult
and out of the way parish where patrons never come,
and where God only knows the work, the life, and

the self-sacrifice,—" Where dost Thou want me to go ? "
How easy it is to sing " Anywhere, everywhere, I
will follow Jesus "—but if we are to teach people to
sing these words from their hearts then must we, as
officers in the fight, have learned to live them out.
When once this lesson is learned, restlessness and un-
settlement, which are so fatal to spiritual fruit,
vanish, and the man of God pursues his work knowing
he is just where his Lord would have him be. He
leaves the so-called " preferment " in the hands of
the Master of the Vineyard knowing that sometimes
in His eyes, the best " preferment " is to be left where
he is.

VI. **The Qualifications necessary for a successful Ministry and their Attainment.**

In the Ordinal men are enjoined to apply themselves
to this " one thing " and " to wax riper and stronger " for
their work, or in other words to aim at being " workmen
who need not to be ashamed," men who are striving
to fit themselves for any and every service to which
their Lord may call them. They are men who desire
to be " the best." They are not like Seneca, whose
ambition was merely to be better than the worst
rather than equal to the best. They realize that they
are meant to possess both power and authority and
that the two do not always go together, as when the
Scribes sat in Moses' seat and had authority but no
power, whereas the Prophets possessed power though
they lacked the authority of the sons of Levi.

The Church commissions her Ministers and gives
to them, in the Name of God, their authority, but
the secret of power they must ascertain for themselves.
Deacon and Priest must remember this, and all through
his Ministry a man must strive to make himself, by

the blessing of God, physically, mentally, and spiritually powerful for the work to which he is called. The wise words of Dr. Pusey to Canon Liddon must be borne in mind "Limit your work." The Christian work must not supersede the Christian life. Time must be arranged, good habits formed, methods of life and work must be laid down if loss is not to ensue.

A word of warning should be raised against the pernicious habit of over-indulgence in sleep and unpunctuality at breakfast on the part of many clergy. Henry Martyn prayed for deliverance from " the sin of lying in bed." Wesley for years made it his habit to rise at four in the summer and five in the winter; the learned Bishop Wordsworth of Lincoln was always to be found in his study at six o'clock. Although times may have changed and the late hours in large towns no doubt affect, in some degree, the question of early rising, yet, much more work can be done, a much better example can be set by acquiring such habits, than by allowing ease and sloth to gain the mastery. Time given to needless sleep, is not only time lost, it is injurious to spiritual influence in the household, for what landlady or servant can possibly respect the " sluggard " or honour him as the devoted servant of that Lord Who arose " a great while before it was day."

(a) *Physical Equipment.*—" The body is the temple of the Holy Ghost " and as such should be maintained in good repair, equally with the fabric called the Church in which the congregation itself offers worship. The body must be brought into subjection so that it may be meet for the Master's use. The man of God must be careful concerning his food and his drink. Time must be given for proper and adequate recreation and exercise. A famous physician recently said, " A

man is more likely to keep well by climbing a tree
than by drinking a concoction made of its leaves."
Walking, cycling, tennis, golf, or fives, with cricket or
football, may be used as helps to the work by maintaining the body in good health and in readiness for
service. The day " off " which every wise Vicar
insists upon his Colleagues taking, should not be merely
the day " off," but used for the special object of
making mind and body perform their duties the better
on the other six days. Therefore the " day off " should
not be used in a casual haphazard manner, but as a
day of preparation and plans for its best use should be
drawn up beforehand.

(b) *Mental Equipment.*—Lord Bowen, speaking to a
number of students of the law, said that " most cases
are really won in chambers." This is equally true
concerning the work of the priest. The famous saying
of St. Francis de Sales that " the knowledge of the
Priest is a Sacrament of the Church " contains a great
truth. " Apt to teach " implies " apt to learn."

To-day the increasing spread of education makes it
all the more incumbent on the Church to see that her
Ministers are men of sound learning. The recent
action of the Bishops with regard to the raising of the
intellectual standard of Ordinands was both wise and
necessary. But if an Arts course is considered a
necessary complement to the training at a Theological
College, it is equally important that the University
career should be followed by definite Theological studies,
and especially is it desirable that " Honours " men,
whose views on many questions may have been disturbed during the course of their reading, should enter
some Theological Hall previous to Ordination.

Suffer a word of counsel and friendly warning.

While up at the University it is well to remember that you are not sent here primarily as Missionaries to evangelize the University and Town. Far be it from me to suggest that no Christian work should be undertaken, and that no help should be given to the Church and her work, but on the other hand I press upon you the importance of realizing that your first, your main object is *preparation* for work, rather than work itself. I have known men who while " up " have so thrown themselves heart and soul into some Church work, that they have gone down without a degree, or with a " pass " degree where Honours might have been theirs. Do such men realize the great injury they are inflicting upon all who come under their Ministry in the years that are to follow ? It means that their Ministry through every year of its duration, is to be of an inferior quality, and that every parish in which they serve is to suffer at their hands. Every student should realize that his duty alike to God and to man demands that his powers during his under- graduate course should be concentrated on " taking in " rather than on " giving out " ; on preparation for the Ministry rather than in the Ministry itself.

But what is to follow Ordination ? Surely not men- tal stagnation begotten by indolence or inattention to reading ? One great purpose of an University course is to train men how to study, to bring their mind under discipline and to teach them to read that which they do not like. If this training is to bear fruit, then the University is to be regarded not as the end of mental preparation but as its beginning. Books are not to be put away and study is not to cease simply because there are no examinations to be passed. The mental grip is not only to be maintained but increased. This cannot be accomplished by the study of a cheap " analysis " or of small handbooks, but by the mastery of the books of the great Divines. The growing number of calls on a Minister's time makes the attainment of mastery increasingly difficult ; but when for example we think of a Gladstone with the burden of Empire on his shoulders, reading annually Homer and Butler, we realize how in the busiest parish something of the kind can be done. The study of Hooker, Butler, Jewel, Pearson, Cranmer, Ussher, Jeremy Taylor, Barrow, Waterland, to mention no modern writers, will tend to make the brain stronger and our thinking clearer and the effect will certainly be felt by our people. A small library of great books is of infinitely more value than a large library of small books. The reading should be wide. It should include Philosophy, Science, Biography, and especially History. Above all, in our reading we must observe a sense of proportion. We, of all men, must preserve the open mind and seek only for the " Truth," and thus we should read all sides whether concerning Theological, Ecclesiastical, Social or Political Questions. For example, Gore's *The Church and the Ministry* should be followed by Lightfoot's *Christian Ministry*, Wordsworth's *Ministry of Grace* by Lindsay's *Church and Ministry in the Early Centuries*, and vice versa. In this way our convictions will be built upon sound premises, and while we may take the side of Broad, Evangelical, or High Churchmanship, we realize that there is another side of the Truth besides that which appeals to us. This will tend to moderate that bitterness and party spirit which is as harmful to the prosperity of the Church as it is to the individual soul. The Christian Minister must never cease to learn as

long as he has people to teach, and he should so live
that what is written at Mentone, over the grave of J. R.
Green, may be said of him, "He died learning."

(c) *Spiritual Equipment.*—After all *the* essential
qualification for the Christian Minister is that of Spiritual power. "Not by might (whether it be that of an
army, organization, or a society) nor by power (whether
it be individual capacity or work) but by My Spirit,
saith the Lord." Samson possessed physical strength,
Solomon mental power, Byron genius, Napoleon organization, but all their lives ended in failure simply because *their* respective powers were not controlled and
guided by the Highest Power of all, the Holy Spirit
of God. Sir Joshua Reynolds was asked by a friend
to view a picture, and anxious as he was to appreciate
the picture, he praised this and that point, until at
last, his sterling honesty made him burst out, "But
after all, it lacks *that*——." His friend knew what
was meant and that the lack of that undefined quality
could never be made up or compensated for. So the
lack of spiritual power in the Minister cannot be
remedied by work, however great, by preaching, however brilliant, by organization, however perfect.

This our Church enforces when it exhorts us to be
wholesome examples to the flock of Christ and to frame
our lives and the lives of our families according to the
doctrine of Christ. How truly Baxter spoke, when
he said that many preachers cut the throat of their
sermons by their lives. We must not merely "lure
to other worlds" but we must "lead the way." We
are in a real sense to be "separated men." "Separate Me Barnabas and Saul." "Separate Me." This is
formally done at our Ordination, but we seldom fully
grasp the number and the power of the enemies of the

Spiritual life of the clergy. Samson " wist not that the Lord had departed from him "—yet he had been dedicated even before his birth to be " God's man," and was known as such. So wherever the Minister of God goes, his very dress differentiates him from other men. He cannot walk in the street, board a train or tram, enter a place of amusement, leave a house, buy in a shop or market, but he is recognized as one *professing* to be " the man of God," and so at every step his spiritual life is challenged. How well St. Paul knew this when he said, " I keep under my body and bring it into subjection lest that by any means when I have preached to others I myself should be rejected." To achieve victory how great must be the daily, nay hourly, fight, against Indolence, Self-indulgence, Pride, Formalism, Jealousy and Censoriousness of others, especially of men in the same Orders as ourselves ! The keenness of the struggle can never be realized fully by any who are outside the Ministerial Office.

The true Shepherd thinks continually of his flock. How will this act of his, this habit of his affect his people ! It may not be a snare to him, but it may ensnare some of them. What of his irritability ? How will it affect the children of the house ? The maid of all work, who listens to his plea on the Sunday night for sacrifice on behalf of Foreign Missions, will not have her own resolutions thereon strengthened if she sees the pipe lighted at all hours of the day and night. Few clergymen realize how they are watched, and how people draw their own conclusions as they witness the difference between the sermon and the life.

Some time ago, the family of a young man who had

been confirmed in my Church, removed from the parish. Some three years later I accidentally met the young fellow and asked him how he was going on. I found he had given up Church, Holy Communion, Prayer and the Bible. After some hesitation he told me the reason. Shortly after their removal his sister married. Just at that time, the Vicar of the Parish was seeking apartments for his Curate, and it was decided that he should come and occupy the vacant room, and the father said to his family, " You must remember the coming of Mr. A. to live with us will make a difference to our house. We have never had ' Family Prayer,' although I have often thought we ought to, but after the way Mr. A. spoke about it last Sunday, he is sure to want us to have it." " Well," the lad went on, " Mr. A. came to live with us. He never once mentioned ' Family Prayer,' he never prayed with us, if we were away from Church and Holy Communion he never asked us the reason for our absence, and when my father was ill he never prayed with him or asked him whether he would like the Holy Communion, so I got disgusted with it all, and although I know I ought not to have done so, I threw everything over and felt I could not go to Church to hear a fellow preach who lived like that." This is one illustration of men " cutting the throat of their sermons by their lives."

Here is another instance. A van driver was a drunkard but had the good sense to keep sober while on duty. Every Saturday and Sunday night for years he had been drunk, with the result that his wife and children were half starved and thinly clad, although the man was earning good wages. One Sunday to his own surprise and to that of everybody else's

he came to my Men's Service. I was led that afternoon to speak of the evils of the Drink Traffic, and
after my address, during a period of silence, I said,
" If there is a man here who has given way to drink
let him, here and now, give it up and say from his heart
' God help me.' " The result was told to me a year
later by the man during a private interview previous
to his Confirmation. He said that as he sat in the pew
and I spoke concerning the drink he said to himself,
" He means me." " That's me." Then all at once I
said, " Here goes, I'll chuck it," and then added, " God
help me," and then he laughed at the very thought of
his doing without the drink. " Well," he continued,
" I went home and did not say anything to my wife,
but that Sunday night was hell to me. For years
and years I had always been drunk. However, I
got through and went to bed and the next morning I
started for my work and it was a job to pass the public
house where I always had my 'nip' in the morning,
but I did, I went and got my horse and van, and my
sheet telling me where I was to go. You might have
knocked me down with a feather, for my first job was
to take a Barrel of Ale to —— Rectory for Mr. B.
Well, I drove to the gate and then I hoisted the barrel
on my shoulder and, as I was carrying it down the steps
I said to myself, ' Well, here's a rum go, yesterday one parson told me to chuck the drink out, and
now another of 'em tells me to bring it in.' Well, I
put the barrel down and gives the servant the book
to get signed, and in a minute or two she comes back
with the book in one hand, and in the other a glass of
ale, and she says, ' Here, Rector says he thought
you'd like a drop.' Well that was near finishing me,
seeing it right under my nose. I was just putting out

my hand to take it, when all at once I thought of what you had said, and I says as quick as I could, ' God help me,' and I ran up the steps as if the devil was after me.'' Then the man sitting in my study added, '' Vicar, if I'd drunk that glass, I'm sure I should never have tried again.'' That man is now one of my most regular and keen communicants.

Just recently I have been round the world, and, on one great liner during the second week out, I said to the chief Engineer (a canny Scot), '' I did not see you at Service last Sunday.'' '' No,'' said he, '' I did not come for I wanted to see, before I came, whether you were one of the whisky-drinking, card-playing set, or not.'' He added, '' I do a bit of both myself, but I want to hear a parson with clean tongue and clean hands.''

How careful we have to be lest we make the weak brother to offend. '' I will eat no meat.'' The principle of this abstention must be extended to preclude, if need arise, many an otherwise innocent action.

Who is sufficient for these things ? If the sin of Achan caused defeat at Ai, how much more must the sin of the negligent Minister cause the loss of spiritual power to his Church and his people. '' Examine yourselves, brethren.'' Let the Ember Days, and especially the anniversary of your Ordination, be days set apart. At such a season let the Ordinal be our companion, and as question after question arises before our eyes, let us give an account of our Stewardship as in His sight. But not merely at such seasons. Night by night the Diary should be written and laid before Him, as a true statement of things done, and things left undone, and the Saturday night should be made a real preparation for the Sabbath, by a retro-

spect of the work of the week. Following such retro-
spection, the weekly reading of the thirty-third chapter
of Ezekiel, with its stern passage, " His blood will I
require at thine hand," should be pondered in our
heart. Have souls been lost during the week by our
negligence ? Surely nothing but the personal realization of the presence of our Lord can enable us to stand
firm, and to complete the task given unto us. Cheyne
once said, " I am better acquainted with Jesus Christ
than with any man I know." Brother Lawrence could
say he was in as great tranquility, when among his
kettles and pans in the kitchen, as when kneeling at
the Eucharist. The secret was that he had cultivated
the habit of realizing the Presence of His Lord. " Lo !
I am with you always," is not merely a good text for
the preacher, it is to be realized by him, something to
be his support, day and night, through good report
and ill. Only in this way can the late Earl Selborne's
words in almost his last address be realized. " Be
Spiritual ! Be Spiritual ! Be Spiritual ! "

How can the Spiritual life, so essential to the ministerial life, be attained and retained ? We find guidance in the Ordinal. " Will you be diligent in Prayer,
and in the reading of the Holy Scriptures . . . laying
aside the study of the world and the flesh ? " Prayer
and the reading of the Holy Scripture are, as Lightfoot
says, " the two pillars of the Pastoral edifice," and
neither can be neglected without disaster to the spiritual
life.

(1) *Prayer.*—" Will you be diligent in Prayer ? "
" Ye have need to pray earnestly," are words in the
Ordinal which reveal the importance which the Church
sets upon this means of grace. " *Diligent* in prayer,"
" pray earnestly." Can such words be used to de-

scribe our prayers ? and yet, what the Well was to the ancient Castle, such prayers are to the soul. If the well was poisoned or ran dry then the gates of the Citadel were soon opened to the enemy, and so, if prayer cease, or is poisoned by formality, then the enemy of souls is soon in possession, and Emmanuel rules no longer in the city of Mansoul. We press, and rightly so, for our churches to be opened daily, but how can parishioners be exhorted by a prayerless Priest to avail themselves of this quiet " closet " ? It is true that the claims of the new type of parochial life are increasing, but even so, woe to that Priest who permits them to crush out of his daily life the hours he once devoted to prayer.

Luther said that he had so much to do that he could not get on without three hours a day for prayer. Wilberforce, the freer of the slave, also set aside three hours a day, viz : from five to six a.m., twelve to one, and from five to six p.m., for the same purpose, while Andrew Bonar declared that, unless he prayed at intervals throughout the whole day, he lost the Spirit of God. When prayer is rightly regarded it will be realized that increased work will demand more prayer, just as the larger factory requires the more power. Without private prayer, public prayers will become cold and formal, and preaching will become as sounding brass or a clanging cymbal. The Minister must be diligent in prayer or become slothful in spirit. Therefore I press upon you to maintain at all costs throughout your ministry your time for prayer. It is essential for your own spiritual development and for the prosperity of the Church of which you are a Minister. If the Master Himself spent the whole night in prayer before calling His Apostles, how much more will it be incumbent upon you to pray concerning every appointment in the Church, whether of curate, churchwarden, or verger ? If Christ prayed for Peter, knowing his weakness and his vacillation, then should not every parish Priest pray, and that earnestly, for the wanderer, the waverer, the weak one of the flock ? The Great Shepherd knows His flock by name, the under-shepherd must also have their names in his heart, especially when upon his knees. To many a Philemon in his congregation he ought to be able to say like the great Apostle, " I thank my God, making mention of thee always in my prayers " (Phil. 4). Preach *to* souls, but also pray *for* souls, for as Augustine taught, " We may not doubt that the end is to be gained far more by the devotion of our prayer than by any power of eloquence." Therefore, whatever else is left undone during the day, the Parish Priest, for the sake of his own soul and the life of his people, will find time for Prayer—for without Prayer who can live ?

(2) *Reading the Holy Scriptures.*—" Will you be diligent in reading the Holy Scriptures ? " There are many reasons for insisting upon the diligent and daily study of the Bible. It contains all things necessary to salvation, and again, as Jerome tells us, " It is the business of the Priest to answer the people's questions about the Holy Scriptures. If he be a Priest, let him study the law of God. If he knows it not, he declares himself to be no Priest, for it is the Priest's office to expound the Scriptures to his people." Even on lower grounds the Preacher will study them for the purpose of increasing his intellectual equipment, and his power in literary expression. He will be wise in following the example of Westcott, and read a book through twice

in English, and once in Greek or Hebrew, as the case may be, before he touches a Commentary, because aids to the study of the Bible must always be " aids " and must never overshadow, or supersede, the study of the Book itself. Again that he may understand the better the principles which underlie the ministerial office and its functions, he will master the teaching given concerning them in the New Testament, and especially in the Pastoral Epistles. But above and beyond all, he will seek, for his own soul's health, inwardly to digest the spiritual food he will find there. Realizing how inseparable is the Word from his Public Worship and Prayer, he will use it in the same degree, in his private devotions, and gradually he will become like Wesley— a man of one book. The best of books will be in his hand and still more in his heart, teaching him the Will of God, comforting him in every sorrow, guiding him in every perplexity. As it was to his Lord, so it will become to him, the armoury where he will ever find a weapon with which to slay his every foe. If you would be a Christian man, far more if you would be a Christian Minister, you must be diligent in reading the Holy Scriptures.

Other books, permeated with the Word of God and known generally as books of Devotion, should be upon your bookshelf, and used by you. Here a word of warning is necessary. Books purporting to be of this kind, have greatly multiplied in recent years and are to be found everywhere. May I urge upon you the importance of largely ignoring them, and using mainly those books which may rightly be termed Classics and have been helpful to thousands. Every Minister should know and value such works as : Augustine's *Confessions*, Bishop Andrewe's *Devotions*, Jeremy Taylor's *Holy Living and Dying* and Law's *Serious Call*. Beyond these, I should be loath to advise, except it be to recommend some excellent works of this description by the present Bishops of Durham and Edinburgh and also Forbes Robinson's Letters.

Once again, in addition to being diligent in Prayers and reading the Holy Scriptures, may I press upon you the incalculable benefits obtainable by the regular and faithful reception of—

(3) *The Holy Communion.*—General Gordon, who was not a member of the Church of England, realized this. In a far-off station, he wrote in his Diary, " There is no eating here and I miss it." It is said that whenever he returned to London from his journeys abroad, he would spend his Saturday night in visiting churches in the West End, that he might discover at what hours the Holy Communion was to be administered, and that he would spend his first Sunday in going from one Celebration to another. This may not be an example which it would be advisable to follow, but it does reveal how greatly Gordon had learned to value this channel of grace to the soul. You cannot neglect to " feed upon Him " in His own appointed way without serious loss to your spiritual life. But care must be exercised, lest even this service becomes merely formal and mechanical. You must strive by prayer and in faith so to communicate, that you may " take this Holy Sacrament to your comfort." It is well at intervals to endeavour to arrange whether you be a Curate or a Vicar to attend the Holy Communion without having to officiate, and, for the purpose of Communion, quietly to take your place among those who are seeking to feed upon Christ by faith.

So, brethren, by Prayer, the Word of God, and the

Holy Communion you will grow riper, stronger for the work to which you are called. You must give yourself wholly to these things, remembering how great is your responsibility as the Minister of God and His Church. It is a greater responsibility than is given to a man in any other calling. If a Captain lose his ship it means much, but if you lose a soul, who can estimate the greatness of the loss? You are responsible to the *World*, for into your charge is given the only balm to heal its wounds, the only message which can dispel its darkness, give it hope, and lead it back to God, and so make of earth a Heaven. You are responsible to the *Church* which in the Name of God has commissioned you to be her teacher and guide, and if " Ichabod " be written over the doors of your Church, it will be to you a shame throughout eternity. You are responsible to *God* Who gave His Son to die for men, and to forgive you and adopt you as His child. He has sent you forth bidding you tell men of their Father's love, and constrain them to return to Him. You are responsible for work done, or left undone, which will affect eternity. How great, how glorious, how awful, is this ministry of yours! " I magnify my office," said St. Paul. You cannot magnify it too much—nay, as you ponder over it in your heart, you may well cry out in alarm, " Who is sufficient for these things? " But listen! And amid the silence, the eternal and loving voice will be heard " Fear thou not, for I am with thee," and, realizing His Presence, His Power, and His Love, you will face your work, stupendously great as it is, with gladness, and confidence, and you will be able to say with St. Paul, " I can do all things through Christ Which strengtheneth me."

LECTURE THE SECOND

In the Congregation

MINISTERIAL work is mainly of a twofold nature, that which concerns the Congregation of the Church, and that which lies in the Parish, among all sorts and conditions of men. The efficiency and the success of the latter depend largely, if not altogether, upon the thoroughness and spirituality of the former. It is therefore of the greatest importance, that everything connected with the Church and her services should be such as would foster the growth and development of spiritual power. Let us first consider the building called the Church and the character of the Service held within its walls.

I. The Building Itself.

The building may be old, and its architecture bad, but if the Clergyman is wise, he will be careful on his first entry into a Parish, not to cause needless pain, dissension and strife, by disparaging a building which, although ugly, is hallowed ground to many within the congregation. There, their parents were married, they themselves were baptized and confirmed; at those rails they knelt in the Holy Communion for the first time, at the Chancel steps they became man and wife, and in God's Acre outside lie the remains perhaps of father, mother, wife, or child. To some, such a building can never be ugly, for it is consecrated by a

24

thousand memories, and woe be to that Minister who lightly jests concerning its being out of date or airily talks of its destruction.

If a new church is desirable the wise Vicar will move carefully, and will aim at carrying his congregation with him, by helping them to realize that the proposed changes are such as are likely to make for greater Christian activity and progress.

Whether, however, the church be old or modern, it must be maintained in good repair and kept scrupulously clean. There can be no excuse for dirt or untidiness. It is right that the House of God should be as beautiful and fair as human hands can make it. We realize that " God is a Spirit," that we are in the new Dispensation, and that it is gloriously true that the God of Heaven can be worshipped in a barn, a kitchen, or an attic, yet surely He who made the mountain, sea, and valley, and has given to us the lily and the rose, and who through His servant has revealed the glory around the Throne, would have His children, with joyful hearts build unto Him, their Lord, a House of Prayer worthy of His Name.

But there must be discrimination, and proportion in all things, and the relative importance of different parts of the Church's work must be considered. Thus it would not only be disproportionate, but disastrous, for ten thousand pounds to be spent on mere decoration, while a mission district is left without a Priest in charge. If the congregation so desire, let there be flowers by all means, but let not your Church be like a Church which is known to me, and which spends fifteen pounds yearly on flowers and contributes little more than two pounds to spread the Gospel among the heathen. Again, if a Cross be introduced, let it not be a cause of dissension and strife. Unfortunately this symbol of our faith has been associated in past days with much that is false in doctrine and harmful to the real development of spiritual worship, therefore men who object to its being used in our churches are not necessarily bigots or narrow-minded. There is much to be said from their point of view, and yet the Cross is that in which St. Paul gloried, and the empty cross always proclaims the finished work of Christ. Again, each one of the Church's children carries the cross signed upon the forehead in Baptism. Surely then, they are not to be condemned, who find in the symbol of the Cross within their church an aid to their worship.

If stained glass windows are put in, let them not be crude in design or inartistic in character. Let them convey some message of the Saviour's life to the congregation. It does not help a congregation to face figures of men placed in windows, and to be unable to discover whether they represent Patriarchs, Prophets, or Apostles. In the East end of my own church there are three windows, depicting the Incarnation, the Crucifixion, and the Resurrection, while in a window above the Saviour is represented as lifting His Hands in blessing while He ascends. Speaking personally, these have been most helpful to me. When I walk up the aisle at a Burial service, repeating the words " I am the Resurrection and the Life," an added meaning comes into the words, as my eyes rest upon the picture of our Lord coming forth from the grave. In considering this question, as all others connected with the church, the Priest must ever remember that the church is not made for him, but he for the church, that he may remain there only for a few years, whereas many of his people will worship there for life. He is bound, there-

fore, to consider the congregation, their wishes and
desires, and nothing should be altered or introduced,
without the consent of an overwhelming majority of
the people. All decorations should be of such a nature
as not to distract the mind, or detract from the
spiritual worship, but to stimulate the devotions of
Minister and congregation, and to make both alike
realize even more fully that they are in the House of
God and at the very gate of Heaven.

II. Ritual.

In these days, with something approaching anarchy
advocated among certain sections of the community, it is most important that the Church,
and specially the Clergy, should set an example
of obedience to law, and should acknowledge the
claims of Authority. That in many respects the
Prayer Book requires revision is generally admitted,
but until such revision has been accomplished by the
Church at large, each clergyman is bound to use the
book prescribed and to use it in accordance with its
directions. He must remember that, while having
something in common with those of the Eastern and
Roman liturgies, the Anglican use is, in many respects,
of set purpose distinct and apart from both, and that
it is not his work or province to introduce into the
worship of the Church any practices which that Church,
as a whole, has deliberately excluded or has, at any rate,
not admitted. The duty of loyalty to the Book of
Common Prayer is emphasized by the fact that it is
the Book of *Common* Prayer, and that members of the
Church have a right to find it in use in every church
in the land which they may enter for the purpose of
worship.

Within the limits of the Prayer Book itself, there is

room for such divergences in public worship as may meet varied temperaments and suit different local conditions, while at the same time preserving the essentials of unity in worship. "Amen" is still "Amen" whether said in St. Paul's, Onslow Square, or sung to Stainer's setting in St. Peter's, Eaton Square. The Psalms are still the Psalms, whether read or chanted. The Creed is still the Creed, whether said or sung. In all such questions it is well to remember—

(a) That true Dignity is often enhanced by Simplicity.

(b) That loyal members of the Congregation should not needlessly be disturbed in their worship by the introduction of numerous changes, even if they are of a non-important nature. For example, the practice of kneeling at a certain place in the Creed does not affect any point of doctrine, although it might be taken by implication to lessen the importance of other parts of the Creed to which like reverence is not paid ; but, apart from any doctrinal significance, it is most distracting to find persons prostrating themselves to the right and left, when others are following the usual custom of standing. It should be remembered, that the Creed is ordered to be said "standing." These may seem petty details ; but they affect the spirit of brotherhood and community in worship, which it is so important should be preserved.

(c) That the man in the street should be considered.

It is not sufficient to say, " This suits the congregation"—I remember these words being said to me by a Minister whose service was the essence of dulness, and whose church was more like a barn than the House of God. If it suited the Congregation, it was apparent that it did not suit the parishioners, for they were not found inside the church. The Congregation, which was so carefully considered, numbered but fifty all told on the Sunday night. A ritual, which, by its deadness and coldness on the one hand, or by its over elaboration on the other, repels the outsider, must ever be avoided.

(d) That no changes should be made without a clear answer in the affirmative being given to such questions as " Will this really assist in pure and spiritual worship ? "   " Will it be such as shall be commonly understood and appreciated, not merely by the priest and a select few of the congregation, but by the people generally ? "

These topics claim attention, although they may appear to some trivial. Clergy, who have had experience of the work in large parishes, know them to be of real importance in many cases.

We must consider now in detail the various parts of Ministerial work inside the church itself, in the midst of the Congregation.

III. **The Minister in the Pulpit.**

" Be thou a Dispenser of the Word of God."   " Take thou authority to preach the Word of God."   These words, used in the Ordinal, together with the fact that a copy of the New Testament is given to the Deacon, and the Bible to the Priest, on their ordination, emphasizes the importance which our Church attaches to the pulpit part of Ministerial work.

This is in full accord with New Testament teaching, for although the Holy Communion, important as it is, is only mentioned in two or three places in the Epistles, yet running right through each Epistle is reference after reference to the " proclamation of the Word."   The Minister is to be the Herald, the Ambassador, the Evangelist, the Witness, the Teacher, the Prophet ; and in carrying out this work, he will follow the example of his Lord, and of the early disciples who went every-where " preaching the Word."

The importance of preaching can scarcely be over-estimated, because upon its spirituality, its scriptural character, and its effectiveness, will depend largely the position and value which the Congregation will place upon the Sacraments, and also the zeal with which they will carry on the real work of the Church. Cyprian says, " By preaching souls are begotten and roused to God, while in the Eucharist they are nourished or healed." Therefore, in the interest of the life of the Church, and that he may be a better " Dispenser of the Sacraments " to a congregation valuing them for their spiritual sustenance, the Priest will remember the words of Phillips Brooks, " Whatever else you count yourself in the ministry, never lose the fundamental idea of yourself as a messenger, saying, " 'Thus saith the Lord.' "

Strong and forceful preaching was never so greatly needed as now. Men have ceased to go to Church, sim-ply from habits of custom, but they will attend, if the Preacher in the pulpit is a Man with the characteristics of a man, and if his word stirs the blood and makes them think, and if they find that they are the better men for his words. Rubertstein voices the opinion of many when he says, " I will go to Church, if you will take me to hear some preacher who will make me try to do the impossible." Is such preaching common in our midst to-day? Is Canon Simpson correct in saying, " The Anglican pulpit can scarcely at the present time be described as either interesting or impressive "? That, in support of this criticism, there is much evidence is only too apparent. Let the visitor to the seaside give his impressions of the preacher, let the labourer on his way home from the village church describe what he has thought and felt during the sermon, let the thoughtful working man put his ideas of the preacher in the local press, let the attendant at a fashionable church state the alterations produced in his weekly doings by the words from the Pulpit. Put these testimonies together, and what will be the result ? Will it not correspond very largely to our own experience, as we think of the few sermons which have really gripped us, conscience and heart alike, and forced us to cry out— " What shall we do ? " It is little wonder that so few men are present in our Churches, when there is frequently so little to inspire them, so little to furnish them with higher ideals or lead them to loftier life and nobler work. It is not sufficient that the sermon is full of instruction. This could generally be obtained with greater advantage by means of a book read quietly at home. The sermon must be one calculated to persuade and move men. It must not only contain food, it must tempt men to eat. It must not only be full of the facts of our Lord's life and teaching, it must move men to come to Him and to carry out His teaching. Therefore, let us consider :—

IV. **The Object of the Sermon.**

Henry Ward Beecher on his deathbed said : " The greatest object of the preacher is not to teach Theology, is not to engage in controversy, but it is to save souls." This was ever the object of the Apostles, and the invariable result of their preaching. We are to expect results from our preaching. Conversions may be sudden or gradual, but conversion must be, or our Ministry is in vain. Some men dislike the attempt to calculate results, and of course an exact estimate is impossible, but when men sneer at the number of " alleged " conversions, it is per-

missible to wonder whether, in *their* Ministry they ever
see such, and whether they have taken the trouble to
notice how careful the sacred writers are to give us
numbers. " Twelve " Apostles ; the " Seventy " ; even
the number fed, " four thousand," " five thousand,"
the baskets, " twelve " ; the number in the Upper room,
" thirteen." " One hundred-and-twenty " ; the number that saw our Lord, " five hundred " ; the number
converted, " three thousand," and again, " five thousand." We see the same reference to numbers in our
Lord's teaching, " one hundred " sheep and " one "
astray ; the " one," " two," and " five," talents, and
what each produced ; the fruit some " thirty," " sixty,"
and " an hundred " fold. Such a scriptural practice cannot be ignored, but when indulged in, it must
be always with the honest desire that for success, God,
and God only, is praised, and for failure man, and man
alone is blamed. " I have planted, Apollos watered,
but God *gave* the increase," and if increase cannot be
seen, it may be taken for granted that something is
wrong either with the planting or the watering.

The object of all preaching is to affect and to alter the
life, by bringing it into closer touch with God through
Christ. The gathering of a crowd is not in itself a sign of
effectiveness in preaching. The great French Preacher
Bayignan said once to Lacordaire : " I hear that
you had such a crowd at your last sermon that the people were sitting *on the top of the Confessionals.*" " Ah !
perhaps," said the other, " but you manage to make
them go *into* the Confessional." The result of our
preaching should be that our people on their homeward
way, do not say, " What a fine sermon ! " but " How
great is the love of God to me ! What can I give to
Him ? What can I do for Him ? " This is the only

effect worth producing. I often wonder, whether the life lived throughout England on the Monday is better, compared with that of the Saturday, owing to the message from twenty-thousand pulpits on the day between. Have people been comforted in sorrow? Have men been aroused from the sleep of sin and death? Have souls been raised to life and stimulated to fight more bravely the battle of life? As you go forth to preach, realize your object and have it clearly in your mind. If you aim at nothing definite, no definite good will result. Dr. Chapman, the well known Mission Preacher, says that he was induced to alter his mode of preaching by the words of Moody to him. " You are making a mistake in your Ministry. What you are doing does not count for much ; your preaching, I say it with all kindness, does not win souls." " Does not win souls ! " then what is it worth? To sum up this part of our subject, may I put the object of a sermon thus :

1st. To win a soul from death by proclaiming Christ, and a free, full, and present salvation through Him.

2nd. To build up men in the Faith, and thus fit them for any work which God may call them to do.

3rd. To make men keen about the work of God and the salvation of men, putting this object before everything else, even before life itself.

Happy will be such a preacher, blessed with results here, and sure of his Lord's " Well done " hereafter.

If this then be the object of preaching let us consider—

V. **The Subject of the Sermon.**

What should it be, in order to achieve this end? It must be the Christ. " I determined to know nothing

D

among you but Christ, and Him crucified." It must be the Gospel, or as Tennyson once called it, "The old news, the good news, the new news." When the pulpit fails, it fails because it either ceases to present the Christ at all or because it presents Him as a Christ, largely divested of His Divinity, and shorn of His saving Power.

Let me warn you concerning three temptations which may beset your path as a Preacher.

(1) The first is to make a sermon what may be called "A Moral Essay." This was where the pulpit failed in the eighteenth century. Blackstone tells us that in 1765 he had heard every preacher in London, and that he did not hear a single discourse which had more Christianity in it than the writing of Cicero, and that it was impossible for him to discover from what he heard, whether the Preacher were a follower of Confucius, Mohammed, or Christ. Is it any wonder that as Butler states: "men had ceased to regard Christianity with any serious consideration at all." That there is such a danger to-day is certain.

During a summer holiday two or three years ago, I heard, in the Church of a celebrated seaside town, a sermon in which the words "Lord," "Christ," "Saviour," "Jesus," "God," were never once uttered. Such a sermon is a profanation and a desecration of the Pulpit. We are sent to proclaim the Christ, the Son of God, and that, believing, men may have life through His Name.

(2) A second temptation of the modern preacher is to present the Christ merely as a Social Reformer, rather than as the Saviour of men. Living as I do in the East End of London, and knowing something from experience of the appalling social evils in our

midst, I am keen, most keen, for Social Reform of the most drastic nature. I know full well from the teaching of the Sermon on the Mount, and from the Parables of our Lord, that Christianity includes all such questions, and that the Christian Minister is bound, even as the Prophets were in ancient times, to speak with no uncertain voice on Social questions. But if the preacher transform his Pulpit into an Election platform, and if the sermon becomes simply and solely concerned with the environment, rather than with the hearts of men, then alas for the prospect of that church being the birthplace of souls into the Family of God. The result of proclaiming a Gospel, dealing simply with environment, will be akin to that produced when great pains are taken to provide beautiful clothes, and adequate provision of food, for a body *in which there is no life*. Let the Preacher who is tempted in this direction take warning from Germany. The growth of Rationalism in that country is largely the result of the eighteenth century preaching, treating almost entirely on the subject of health and industry. The Preacher must aim first and foremost, and all the time, at putting right the environment, *through* the regeneration of the man, and not preach as though he can regenerate the man by putting right the environment. The " New Birth," and the " New Birth " alone, will lead to the Regeneration of the World.

(3) Again, the Preacher may be tempted to bring forward too prominently difficulties concerning " Belief," and controversies which rage around Faith. Such difficulties must be met, and the attacks on the Faith cannot be dismissed altogether with studied disdain. More will be said on this question when discussing another branch of our subject (*see* Chapter V),

but it is well to remember that a sermon full of mere negation, is as certain to fail in moving the congregation as would the policy of any political party in appealing to the electorate on such a basis. The presentation of the positive side of Truth is the best method of exposing and expelling error. To be always preaching on " Doubt," is one method of inculcating " Doubt." Dr. Samuel Johnson once said : " Men get tired of hearing the Apostles tried once a week for forgery; their souls long for better food." Above all, as Dr. Dale so well warns the Preacher, beware of writing a sermon which may clear your own mind, but fog those of your hearers." What men desire to-day is positive preaching by men who believe, with all their hearts, in Christ as their Lord and Saviour. Men must speak concerning the controversies of men, from the standpoint of those who possess a personal knowledge of their Lord, and as those who, in the Isle of Patmos, have seen the Vision. Such are men who remove " Doubts" far sooner than they of the school of Logicians. Let a man be able to say, " I have seen the Babe of Bethlehem, and declare unto you that in Him God is linked with manhood for ever "; " I have seen Him of Calvary, and proclaim Him to you sinners "; " I have looked into ' the Grave,' and declare unto you that mourn that ' He is risen,' and because ' He is risen, your dead will rise again ' "; " I have gazed into the Heaven, and have seen Him watching the world, interceding for men, waiting to return for His own, that where He is, they may be also; nay, I have heard the Lord saying unto me : ' I stand at the door and knock ': I ' opened ' and He has ' come in,' and He ' sups with me, and I with Him.' " Let a man so preach, and, I say, just as the first sermon preached by St. Andrew, full of the ring of personal conviction, " We have found the Christ," did its work, and brought its hearer to Christ, so will the effect of such preaching be, that its hearers will be brought to the Lord.

The theme of the Preacher then is " the Christ," and his textbook " the Bible." Both are inexhaustible. Both are ever new. Both can be made to live in the pulpit, and in the pew, for both were given to men. But, you say, " Will Doctrinal sermons hold men, grip men, help men ? " If you would know the answer to such a question, buy a volume of the Sermons of Dale, of Newman, of Spurgeon. Read those, by Dale, on the *Atonement, Ephesus, The Church*. Master those, by Newman, on *Saving Knowledge, The Glory of God, Holiness Necessary for Future Blessedness*. Make yourself familiar with Spurgeon, on *the Glory of His Grace, Forgiveness of Sins, Accepted in the Beloved*. Those sermons are at once pastoral, evidential, doctrinal, and evangelistic to the core. The great texts of the Bible would not be great without the doctrine enshrined within them, and the Preacher who does not proclaim the Christ, the centre of all doctrine, is preaching that for which he received no commission, and that which can neither bring peace to the sinner, nor holiness to the life of the Believer.

Such a sermon is not easily forthcoming. Let us then proceed to discuss :

VI. The Making of a Sermon.

It is well to bear in mind the saying of Emerson that, " the first virtue of an Orator is to be interesting." Good food, badly cooked and badly served, neither stimulates the appetite, nor becomes easily digestible, so a Sermon must not only contain good matter, but it must be served in such a manner as will arrest the congregation, and tempt it to eat. A dull sermon makes a sleepy congregation, and, therefore, if your sermon is to be effective, it must be, from beginning to end, interesting. Again, a sermon, when finished, must prove that you yourself understand the subject. When I was a *very* young preacher, I was called upon to preach in a small country village one Sunday afternoon, and thinking that I must preach a sermon suitable to such a district, I selected " The Parable of the Sower " as my subject. After the Service, a good old farmer came into the Vestry to take me home to tea. His reception was not very encouraging, and for a while we walked along the country lane in silence. I then felt a hand on my shoulder, and heard words like the fire of a " Gatling " gun, shattering all my pride in what I thought had been a very well-prepared sermon. " Young man, if ever thee preaches that sermon again, preach it in the towns where they know ' nowt ' about it." Needless to say, that sermon was never preached again, either in town or country. The subject must be mastered, before an attempt is made to teach it. This will involve work. Faith never encourages laziness. " I want more faith," said one, to Richard Cecil. " No," he replied, " more work and more pains." " My leanness, my leanness," on the lips of many preachers should be " my laziness, my laziness." Is it possible to take too much pains, or to work too hard over the preparation of a sermon, when it is realized what the sermon is intended to accomplish, and what are its infinite possibilities ?

First, the " Text." The selection of a Text has been the custom for some seven hundred years, although previously a " Text," as understood to-day, was practically unknown. The custom is a good one, and should not be lightly abandoned, but it must not degenerate into a peg, upon which to hang a number of disjointed thoughts and inane anecdotes. Let it be the keynote of the message from God Himself. When found, do not be in a hurry to ascertain what everybody has thought about it, but rather look at it yourself. Read it in the original. What does it mean? Remember the Fathers had no Commentaries. They simply had the Word itself, and they wrote that which lives to-day. It is well to follow their example, and first to find out what light the Bible throws upon the text. This strengthens and develops a man's own power of thought. Then, and not until then, should the shelf be consulted. The advice of Jean Paul Richter is excellent. " Never read until you have thought yourself hungry, and never write until you have read yourself full." But what class of Book should be consulted? As to Commentaries, I strongly advise the plan of *building* up a Commentary on the whole Bible, by purchasing the best on each individual Book—such as Lightfoot on *Galatians*, Westcott on *St. John*, Armitage Robinson on *Ephesians*—in preference to the purchase of a complete Commentary on the whole Bible. Certain volumes of the *Expositor's Bible* are excellent, and for handy reference the Portable Commentary (two volumes) by Faussett together with the " Century Bible," will be found useful. Commentaries and volumes of sermons wisely used should produce a threefold benefit ; they should add to what you had already thought ; they should modify some of your views, and they ought to have extended others.

Now that your matter has been obtained, turn your attention from your sermon to your people. Consider their characteristics, because a sermon whose arrangement and style would draw one kind of congregation, might possibly repel that of another kind. You will find it an advantage to make an Analysis of your Sermon. The divisions may not necessarily be announced to your people, although there is much to be said in favour of such a course, but they must be clear to the mind of the preacher. With the Analysis completed, a time-table might be arranged, so that each part may have, according to its importance, an allotted time, otherwise the " Introduction " may outweigh and hurry the " Application." This will raise the question as to the length of the Sermon. The craze for short sermons must be resisted. How can the great theme of the Atonement be even touched upon in ten minutes ? If we name the Preachers who have moved men to great lives and deeds, we shall find that not one of them will be found to have been a " Ten Minutes " preacher. No Political Speaker or Social Reformer would for one moment be expected so to restrict himself. If there is a call for " Short " sermons, the fault is not so much in the pew, as in the pulpit. What is wanted is not so much " Shorter " Sermons, as " Better " Sermons. There is a humorous warning in the Bishop of Auckland's conundrum : " Why is a preacher like a camel ? Because he goes on and on and does not know how dry he is." The length must be regulated by the subject, by common sense, and by the guidance of the Holy Spirit.

In the making of your sermon dwell upon *one* great theme. It may be of a Topical, Textual, or Expository character, but let its character be apparent all through the sermon from beginning to end. Do not overload the sermon with too much matter. Work in, and round, and over, and under the One Truth you wish to press home. So our Divine Teacher taught. The illustration of the lilies which toiled not is only a reiteration of the same thought which He wished to convey by His allusion to " the birds of the air." " Without a parable spake He not unto them," and a telling, attractive, brief story is frequently of great use, as any one who reads the sermons of many great preachers will speedily realize. But it is well to remember in this connection, that the best stories are Bible stories, and any one who heard Moody will never forget how he made them live. On the other hand a Sermon with too many stories is weakened thereby. Ruskin's words concerning Art can well be applied to this subject. " When Art sets up as the end of its own existence, and not as the handmaid of Truth, or a spur to duty, it loses its function." So do illustrations. The sermon must appeal to the conscience, but above all to the heart. The Preacher who disdains the effect produced on the emotions, and objects to what is called " emotional " preaching, little realizes that he is slighting that which is of the greatest possible help when rightly used. Of course, there is the wrong way of doing this, as there is a wrong, as well as a right way of reasoning, but it must be remembered that it is " with the heart " that man believeth ; " If thou shalt believe in thine heart . . . thou shalt be saved." Let the Preacher read " His Mother's Sermon " in *Beside the Bonnie Briar Bush* (Ian Maclaren) and he will realize the truth of all this. The introduction of the Sermon must be brief and striking, and the ending solemn and impressive. Let your " Finally " be final. Do not prolong the ending, neither let it be too abrupt. The end of the Sermon must be the application of the

Truth stated as to each individual person in the Congregation.

How did Wesley draw twenty thousand colliers together at five o'clock in the morning, to hear such doctrinal sermons as will be found in his published works ? Surely, under the Holy Spirit's Power it was the " application " which did its work and made men turn from sin to God. This was simply following the example of the great Apostle to the Gentiles in his Epistle to the Romans, where, after eleven chapters of close reasoning on Sin, the Fall, the Atonement, and Justification by Faith, he immediately applies the Doctrine to the practical life. " I beseech you present your bodies a living sacrifice." This is the end of all preaching, the dedication of the life of the hearer to God. The preacher who wishes to produce this effect must be as earnest as St. Paul. " Simeon is earnest," said Wilberforce of the great preacher of Holy Trinity, Cambridge, and it must be said by hearers to-day of a Preacher, if he is to be successful. Such a Preacher must not only prepare his sermon, but also prepare himself. A sermon cannot be prepared like a lecture on chemistry. The latter can be prepared and delivered with effect by a Lecturer full of pride or jealousy, but not so the effective sermon. " God is a Spirit, and they that worship Him must worship Him in Spirit and in truth." May we not add, and they that proclaim Him also, must proclaim Him in Spirit and in truth. The man thus anointed by the Holy Spirit, not merely on his Ordination Day, but also in his study as he prepares, and in his pulpit as he preaches, will find that the Word will not return void, but accomplish that which the Master pleases.

VII. The Delivery of The Sermon.

The sermon has not only to be prepared, it also has to be delivered. Some one has said that half the learning and study of Preachers is useless owing to the lack of proper delivery and pronunciation. Probably this is an exaggeration, but it is certainly true that frequently the delivery renders the sermon very largely ineffective for the purpose for which it was prepared. This is mainly due to the unmanly and unnatural voice, which some preachers seem to suppose is the " correct " tone for the Pulpit. I cannot imagine how any man can think that it is right to speak in drawling singsong tones of the sin of man, the love of God, and the things Eternal. The difference between the tone frequently used in the home, on the platform, and in the pulpit is most marked. Yet of all three, the latter ought to be the most manly, the most earnest, and the most real. Every Candidate for Holy Orders should receive lessons in Voice Production, if not in Elocution. The former is most important if the Speaker is to be preserved from " Clergyman's Sore Throat." The Preacher should speak rather than declaim. His whisper, like that of Pitt in the House of Commons, should be audible to every one. He should learn to understand the value of a Pause, when rightly used. Froude, in a description of Newman as a Preacher, says that Newman, who was at that time Vicar of St. Mary's, Oxford, had been describing some of the incidents of our Lord's Passion. " At this point," Froude says, " he paused. For a few moments there was a breathless silence. Then in a low, clear voice, of which the faintest vibration was heard in the farthest corner of St. Mary's, came the words : ' Now, I bid you to recollect that He to Whom these things were done was Almighty God." It was as if an electric stroke had gone through the church . . . I suppose it was an epoch in the mental history of more than one of my Oxford contemporaries."

The Preacher should watch his actions and his habits of gesture lest, like Colonel Prim, he " strikes an attitude " ; and he should remember that the pulpit is not made to lean over, but to stand in. These may seem trivial matters ; but they are of the greatest importance. Above all the Minister should seek to follow in his preaching the ideal laid down by Holman Hunt concerning his own work. " What I sought," said the great painter, " was the power of undying appeal to the hearts of men." Could Preachers have a better ideal ? " The power of undying appeal to the hearts of men." May we never preach without this spirit filling our heart and resting upon our tongue.

What of extempore Preaching and the reading of Sermons ? Sermons were not read until after the Reformation, and even then more so in England than on the Continent. The written sermon has the advantage that it is carefully prepared beforehand, and can be made more precise, and probably more clear in expression. Yet even as early as the days of Charles II we find it unpopular, as witness the proclamation issued by that notorious King to the University of Cambridge, in which he strongly condemns the reading of sermons and bids the practice cease. That proclamation has never been cancelled. The famous Dr. Dollinger, in a letter to Mr. Gladstone, said : " Depend upon it, sir, if the Church of England is to make way and be a thoroughly National Church, the Clergy must give up the practice of preaching from written Sermons." Newman said : " For myself, I think it is no extravagance to say that a very inferior Sermon delivered without book answers the purpose for which all Sermons are delivered more perfectly than one of great merit if it be written and read." It is true that some men, like Liddon and Farrar, were effective as Preachers, although they habitually read their sermons, but the majority of preachers had better leave their manuscript outside the pulpit. No politician would ever face a large audience and read his address. The Extempore Sermon gains more than it loses in its ease, directness and vigour. The great danger of such preaching is that the man who has the " gift " of speech may be tempted to rely upon it and to become careless in his preparation, whereas the really effective Extempore Sermon requires as much, if not more, preparation than the written one. A Preacher, especially in his early days, will derive great benefit from writing his sermons, although he may not read them. The evil habit of memorizing must never be encouraged. As men advance in years the difficulty of such a method is increased. Notes of the sermon may, in the first instance, be used, but even with regard to these it is perhaps well to do without them. Dr. Parker for ten years of his ministry wrote and read his sermons, then he used notes for a period, and during the later years of his ministry used none. But whatever his method may be, it will repay any preacher to study the style of men like Addison, Newman, Bunyan, and the speeches of that distinctively Anglo-Saxon Orator, John Bright. I would also recommend the sermons of Latimer (a Prince of Preachers), Tillotson, Barrow, Jeremy Taylor, Wesley (the first fifty-three), and the sermons of more modern preachers such as Liddon, Spurgeon, Maclaren, Dean Church, Parker, Phillips Brooks, F. W. Robertson, Jowett, W. L. Watkinson. Good examples of Mission

Sermons are to be found in the works of the Bishop of London, D. L. Moody, Canon Hay Aitken, Gipsy Smith, and the Rev. Paul Bull.

Important as the work of the Minister is in the pulpit, it is only one of many duties which he has to perform amid the Congregation. He has to be their leader in Worship, in Praise, and Prayer, and to them he has not only to preach about the Word of God, but to read it. Therefore let us consider :—

VIII. The Minister at The Prayer Desk and Lectern.

(*a*) *At the Prayer Desk.*—If the Priest would be faithful and earnest here, he must never regard his work simply as " Taking Duty." The rule of St. Benedict provides that the weekly reader, when he enters on his duty, kneels before each of his brethren, and asks for their prayers. If the preacher requires preparation by Prayer, so equally does the man at the Prayer Desk need to cry : " Lord, teach me to pray." His attitude in prayer must not be slovenly, he must not lounge ; he must *kneel.* He, together with the congregation, are about to lift up his voice to the Lord. That everything in the Service may be rendered with reverence and in order, he should thoroughly master the rubrics. He should know where he is to speak with " a loud voice," and should not make mistakes in announcing the Psalms. He should not have to consult the Calendar to see whether it is a Saint's Day, or even which Sunday it is. He should know, *before* he enters the Prayer Desk, exactly what he has to do. He should remember that he is " *to read* " the Sentences and " *to say* " the Exhortation. The reverse is frequently done. The Prayers are to be *read.* Bishop Gore has condemned, and rightly so, the tyranny of the note G. How much that particular " Note " and the habit of monotoning are responsible for what is known as the Clergyman's sore throat can scarcely be realized, but frequently they cause quite as much harm to spiritual worship. It is well to learn to use the lips and to spare the throat ; to read distinctly, and with a full voice, to hurry nothing, and yet not to dawdle. Read the Collects, which are the masterpieces of the devotion of the ages, in the spirit which they breathe, and if this is done there will be no lip-service, but that which will raise the soul to God.

The Priest is to lead, not only in the prayers, but also in the Worship and Praise. Very rarely now are the Psalms or Te Deum said in our churches (although the rubric gives full permission to do so), but where they are said, the Priest should read his portion with feeling and expression. Generally, however, the conduct of Divine Worship is largely transferred from the Clergy to the Choir ; and with regard to this question great care must be taken lest " Worship by the Choir " be substituted for " Worship by the Congregation." It is frequently asserted that the Choir, if they are to be retained, must have something to do which will exercise their musical ability. Much of this difficulty will, however, be removed if the Organist and Choirmaster are spiritual men, for it is no more right to have an unspiritual conductor of Praise in the choir because he is a good musician, than it is to have an unspiritual man in the Desk to lead the Prayers because he has a good voice. The claims of both the congregation and the choir can be met by singing the " Anthem " in the place appointed, while by chanting to easy settings the Psalms, Canticles, and the Versicles, the Service will be thoroughly congregational. This is most important in working-class parishes, and especially so at the Evening Service, where it is well to provide Prayer Books and to add the number of the page when announcing the Day of the Month and the number of the opening Psalms.

(b) *At The Lectern.*—There are few duties of the Parish Priest which are more important than that of reading the Word of God. It was a task performed by our Lord Himself in the Synagogue at Nazareth and one which must never be undertaken lightly. " Then shall he read distinctly and with an audible voice." " He shall so stand, and turn himself as he may best be heard of all such as are present." Such are the directions in the Prayer Book, and, it is well worth noting, that such reiterated directions are not given elsewhere regarding any other duty entrusted to the Minister. This reveals the importance which our Church attaches to the reading of Holy Scripture. It is still true that " the entrance of Thy Word giveth light," and many have found *the Light* during the reading of the Lesson, even as Bishop Ryle (the first Bishop of Liverpool) did, when he heard the words read, " By grace are ye saved through faith."

The Church directs the congregation to stand during the reading of the Gospel in the Communion Office, thus rendering honour to the very words of Christ the King, but is sufficient reverence paid when the same words are read at the Lectern ? Is it not an act almost verging on sacrilege, to read such stupendous statements as " *God so loved the World,*" " *Come unto Me and I will give you rest,*" in the same tone as the words, " Here endeth the Lesson." When Ezra read he gave the sense, the meaning, and every Lesson should so be read, that, no matter how feeble the Sermon, or inferior the music, every person in the congregation should be made to realize that it was worth an effort to come to church, for they had heard " The Voice of the Lord their God."

But again, at his Ordination the Priest is charged to be " a faithful Dispenser of the Holy Sacraments "— the one Sacrament to mark the beginning of the Christian's life in the Church, and the other to provide spiritual food for its sustenance and growth.

IX. The Minister at the Font.

We do well to remember the importance of Holy Baptism. It was ordained by Christ Himself. That in itself is sufficient to give to it a peculiar and sacred character. Its administration must never degenerate into merely that of " taking Baptisms," but it must be maintained on an equality with the other Sacrament of Christ's ordaining. What the Holy Table is in the Holy Communion, the Font must be in Holy Baptism. If the former Service demand reverence and care in administering, so equally does the latter.

(a) *The Baptism of Infants.*—The Baptism of Infants presents one of the most difficult problems of Church life to-day. Suggestions for its solution cannot be dealt with here.

The bringing of children to Baptism by ungodly people, who ignore the rule of the Church regarding Sponsors, the very general absence of fathers from the Baptism of their children—these are disquieting features of the Public Baptism of Infants as it is administered to-day. Clergy who feel that they cannot refuse this Sacrament to the children of such parentage, administer it with a very heavy heart.

In the Greek and Latin Churches one Godparent is required, but in our Church since the Restoration three have been required. Canon XXIX, which provides that Godparents, other than the parents, must

B

be Communicants, was modified in 1865 by the Convocation of Canterbury so as to permit parents themselves to stand surety for their offspring.

It is well to commence the Service by asking for a brief period of silent prayer on behalf of the children and the parents. Cards containing a copy of the Service should be in the hands of each Adult. It is important that the homily at the end of the Service should be read, and if possible, a two or three minutes' Address should be given explaining the Service and pointing out that the mere teaching of the Creed, the Ten Commandments, and the Lord's Prayer is not all that is expected; but that the Child must be taught what these represent, viz.: Faith, Obedience, and Communion with God. Great care should be taken in filling up the particulars required in the Register. A wrong entry frequently causes in after life much inconvenience. The presentation of a Baptismal Card suitable for framing will give an opportunity later on for the visitation of the parents when their responsibility can be plainly pointed out and the meaning of the Service can be more fully explained. In some parishes a Guild of Sponsors has been formed with excellent results.

(b) *The Baptism of Adults.*—The preparation for the Baptism of Adults requires the utmost care, and the Prayer Book directs that the Bishop shall be informed at least a week before the Sacrament is administered to an adult. The person concerned must be like the Eunuch or the Philippian Jailer, one who believes on Christ as his Saviour. Though classes may be held for the purpose of preparation, yet it may be said that in the case of adults it will be the influence wielded in private interviews which will be likely to produce the deepest impression. Adult Baptism should be followed as soon as possible by Confirmation. This appears to be the Scriptural order, but if this cannot be arranged for some time, it should be remembered that the Rubrics allow the Communion to be administered to those " who are ready and desirous to be confirmed," and the baptized adult should be put in a position to receive the Holy Communion at the earliest possible time.

Candidates for Holy Baptism have the full right to request that they may be immersed. In some localities this is a difficulty, but the plain direction of the Prayer Book demands that no matter how difficult, means must be found to grant the request. In several churches in London (Lambeth and Marylebone for instance) arrangements have been made whereby Baptism by immersion can take place. The Incumbents of such parishes are always willing to afford every facility to any Clergyman who may apply for the use of their special Baptistery.

X. The Minister at the Lord's Table.

To the Priest the Holy Communion will ever mean much. Not one title for it will convey all that it means to him. " The Lord's Supper," " The Holy Communion," " The Breaking of Bread," " The Holy Eucharist," will each have their place in his thoughts, but, whatever the title, it will be to him a Service in which he goes forth to meet and receive his Lord, the Bread of Life. It will be well to realize—

(a) The peculiar and great danger which may beset the Celebrant. From the nature of his Office he has to partake of this Sacrament more frequently than the laity, and thus familiarity may tend to formalism and professionalism. *He has to Celebrate, he has to receive.*

he has to administer, whether he be ready or unready, prepared or unprepared. The danger of this to the spiritual life is apparent. If the laity are warned lest they " eat and drink unworthily," how much more is the warning necessary for the Clergy. If the laity are bidden to examine themselves, how incumbent is the duty upon the Clergy. Although the Articles teach that the unworthiness of the Minister does not make the Sacrament invalid, yet surely his faith, his prayer, will help to make it of greater blessing to his flock. Who can estimate the loss to the Celebrant through unfaithful reception ! The danger is great. " Watch and pray, lest ye enter into temptation," should be in the mind of every Priest as he goes forth to his sacred work.

(*b*) The importance of reverence, reality and faith. Whatever view may be taken of the mode of the Presence of Christ in this Sacrament, all sections of the Church agree that the *Presence is Real*, real from the time the first words " Our Father " are uttered until the last note of Praise ascends at the close. It is the *Lord's* Supper, the *Lord's Table* all the time, and He, at once the Host, and the Feast, is not for one moment absent. Therefore " put off thy shoes from off thy feet, for the place whereon thou standest is Holy Ground." Without reality and faith the Service will become cold, formal and ineffectual.

Points to Remember.

1. That it is the Lord's Supper, therefore let everything be done decently and in order. Things which may seem minute and even trivial must be watched. The Sacred Vessels and the Linen should be kept scrupulously clean. Although not named in the Communion Office, the necessity for a Credence Table is implied by the ordering of the " Bread and Wine " to

be placed upon the Holy Table at a certain part of the Service. At other times the Credence Table can be used for the Alms Dish.

2. There is one observation which may seem an almost impertinent one; yet it is one not altogether unnecessary. The hands of the Celebrant should be newly washed. Again the Celebrant should wear boots which will not creak or make much clatter, and he should learn to move quietly from one Communicant to another.

3. The Sacred Elements should be treated with reverence, for they represent the Body and Blood of Christ, and consequently they also represent the Sacrificial Offering of the Lord Jesus Christ for the Redemption of the world.

4. It is the People's Communion as well as the Priest's, for, as Bishop Creighton said, one great result of the Reformation was to turn the Mass into a Communion. The Holy Communion should be administered in such a manner as to keep in view the essential object of the Service, that of individual souls communing with and receiving their Lord. The aspect of this Communion of the faithful one with another will not be lost sight of. The individual reception of Christ's Body and Blood points to the advisability of administering to each Communicant separately, if this can be done without unduly prolonging the Service. The Words of Administration should be said softly and yet distinctly, and a marked change of voice should characterize the passing from the first half to the second half of the " Words " used. The first is a prayer, " Preserve thy body and soul "; the second is an exhortation, " Feed on Him."

5. The Celebrant should remember that as an almost

imperceptible particle on the lens of a telescope may cause the novice to think that he is beholding a " Spot," so a very small disarrangement of the Service or the introduction of some possibly harmless practice may be, to some worshipper, something which looms large in his eyes, and may become a " Spot " indeed. It is well, therefore, to keep to the Prayer Book Service as directed, whether musically rendered or not, and thus, although men of extreme views on either side may not have the Service exactly as they desire, no loyal Churchman can complain, provided that the Service is performed reverently, orderly, and devoutly. The Presence will then be felt, and it is That for which men will come, it is That which their hearts desire.

6. Communicants should be exhorted to leave the church quietly, and not to loiter near the door, but to go home thoughtfully, and yet joyfully, for they have seen the Lord.

XI. The Minister at other Services.

(a) *Daily Services*—In every parish provision should be made for any one to find a quiet place in which to get alone with God, so every church should be open daily for private prayer. The more crowded the parish the greater the need. But the church should also be open daily for *Public* Prayer. The rubric may, or may not, make the daily use of Morning and Evening Prayer compulsory (personally I think that it does), but there can be no doubt that its helpfulness is a sufficient justification for such use becoming the rule of the Church. Frequently the statement is made— " What is the use ? No one comes." But were our Lord's " lonely " prayers of no use ? Did no benefit accrue to Joshua and his host because there were only two with Moses on the Mount ? Do Clergy who neglect

Daily Prayer realize that its benefits are not confined to the one, two or three who attend, but that its influence can be made to extend to the World at large, and especially to His Church in action, in the midst of the counting-house, the factory, the pit and the shop ? But, says one, cannot the same object be achieved by prayer in the Study ? In one way " yes," in another " no " ; Prayer in the church carries with it associations which count for much. Some little time ago, a man, whose great weakness had been drink and temper, found Christ and was confirmed. Shortly afterwards, in reply to a question as to how he was going on, he said : " The other day I nearly fell, but just at the moment I thought, ' How can I do this thing when I know the Vicar prayed for me this morning on the very spot where I said " I do," ' " and he said, " when I thought of that I didn't give way." The Joshua in the parish is strengthened by the thought of the Moses in the church. But for Daily Service to be helpful in this direction, the people must be instructed concerning its widespread influence, in order that the weary woman tied to her home, equally with the lad out at work for the first time, may gain encouragement from the fact that the Church offers prayer without ceasing on their behalf.

(b) *Holy Days.*—On these the Services are not optional ; they are obligatory. How the Clergy of some three thousand churches in which there are no Services on the days appointed reconcile this neglect with their duty is not clear. Surely, for instance, the life of St. John, the beloved of the Lord, the writer of the Gospel, the Book of the Revelation and the Epistles which bear his name, is one for which the Church should thank God ? It is also one from which the Church through all the ages can gather many lessons and real inspiration. So with all the Saints Days, each has its lesson, and each forms a link which can be ill spared in the chain which connects us with the Apostolic Church.

(c) *Festivals and Seasons.*—It is most unfortunate that the State has seen fit to order a Public Holiday on the day following the great Festivals such as Christmas, Easter, and Whitsun, for this has tended to make these seasons simply a public holiday. Such action should cause the Church to make greater efforts to maintain the spiritual character of these Holy Days. The great Doctrines which are enshrined in the teaching associated with such days as Ascension, Good Friday, the first Sunday in Advent, can never be overlooked without most grievous loss to the Church.

The penitential season of Lent, and especially Holy Week, should be used for Mission Services characterized by great solemnity. The whole congregation should be taught the importance of attendance at the special Services arranged, and there should be a distinct call to Repentance, Faith and Consecration. In many churches during these seasons, at the close of Evening Prayer, the congregation is asked to remain to a short "After Service" at which definite consecration to God is urged. When wisely conducted such gatherings are most helpful in building up the Faith of some and leading prodigals back to the fold.

Marriages—Churchings—Burials.

Before conducting any of these services for the first time a Clergyman should carefully watch some experienced Priest perform the duties of his Office.

(d) *The Marriage Service.*—This Service is the most difficult for the novice to conduct because of its many parts and of its ritual. It is also the most difficult of all services in which to preserve the Spiritual atmosphere. Amid the higher ranks of Society, fashion; dress, the presence of thoroughly worldly people frequently combine to make this solemn Service that of merely a "Society function." Among the working classes the same tendency is observable with the addition that *the* Day is also marked as a holiday on the part of the relatives and friends. The whole street is interested, and the crowd gathers, and "Confetti" bags are got ready. Yet the Ceremony to be performed, whether in Mayfair, or Spitalfields, is one of the greatest importance, so the Clergy must make every effort to maintain the high ideal of Marriage, and as a step towards this, endeavour must be made to make the Marriage Service reverent, impressive, and spiritual. The Officiating Clergyman must be prepared for any untoward event. Tact must be used in dealing with the crowd, and also with the persons concerned; for instance, the girl who laughs and giggles, often does so owing to sheer nervousness, rather than from irreverence. Sometimes an Address may be more helpful than the reading of the Homily. After the Service the Register should be filled in most carefully, and the opportunity seized to express the hope that the newly married couple may often be found in the church in which they have been married. A visit to the home within a few weeks is desirable, and may result in much good.

(e) *Churchings.*—This Service should be solemn and impressive. It is well for the Minister to stand near to the kneeling woman and to read the service in a low and sympathetic voice. If there are signs of mourning it is well not to ask concerning the Child, as it may have died, but otherwise, ere the Mother leaves the church, she should be asked when she intends to bring the Child to be baptized.

(*f*) *Burials.*—In the country parish with " God's Acre " around the church, the Office for the Burial of the Dead is comparatively an easy matter, but in the town parish, especially in a London one, it is complicated, by the distance between the parish and the Cemetery being frequently as much as seven or eight miles. It is impossible for the Clergyman to devote several afternoons a week to this work ; but a most useful practice is that of offering the Parish Church, free of charge, to *any parishioner* for the purpose of taking the first part of the Service. This occupies but a little time, and yet it brings the local Clergy into touch with the mourners, and gives relatives and friends who could not travel the distance to the Cemetery an opportunity of being present. In a populous district frequently a crowd of sightseers will gather. This opportunity of speaking to those who are rarely seen in church should not be lost. If possible a hymn should be sung and an address given.

Some few years ago a girl was murdered in my parish under circumstances which caused me to anticipate a crush, and so it proved. For over an hour before the time for the Funeral Service in church the streets in the vicinity were impassable except for the narrow passage kept clear by the police. I had the doors of the church opened, and in a few minutes it was crowded, galleries and all, with a mixed gathering of men and women who had come from all parts of the East End. Hymn-books were given out and two hymns sung, then followed a prayer, an address, hymn, another address, and so for an hour I conducted a real Mission Service, breaking down prejudice, stilling the excitement, and bringing the people to realize the Presence of Christ. By the time the body of the murdered girl was brought in, the Congregation was moved to a higher plane, and from being sightseers they were ready to become Worshippers. I had reasons afterwards to believe that the Mission Service conducted under such peculiar circumstances had been blessed of God to many present.

A visit to the home before the funeral, and also a few days afterwards, may produce real and lasting results.

But who is sufficient for these things ! Our strength is to be found in the fact that " wherever two or three are gathered together *He* is in the midst." Let this be realized, and whether it be in the Daily Service, or amid the joy of a day spent in Cana, or in the darkness and sorrow of a house in Bethany, the Minister of Christ will have the right word and the right tone, for it shall be given him what he shall say.

The Minister in the Congregation ! What is he like ? Look at the Congregation and he will be revealed. Is it alive, keen, anxious to help forward the time when the Lord shall come ? If such is the case, then you may know that the Minister is a Man of God, one who knows how to pray, who knows the Will of God from His Word, who has learned how to feed upon His Lord in his heart by faith and with thanksgiving. But if, on the other hand, the Church is listless, asleep, dead, then woe to that man who has neglected His Lord's Vineyard, his Candlestick will be removed out of its place, and he, the Lord's Anointed, shall be a castaway as Saul on the mountain of Gilboa, or as Samson in the house of Dagon. From such a fate let our prayer ever be " Good Lord deliver us."

LECTURE THE THIRD

In the Parish

THE preparation for the Ministry should be such as to fit the Minister to be truly a Pastor who knows his sheep, and one who is able to influence those that are outside the fold. He need not aim at being a specialist. There is a place in the Ministry, as there is in Medicine, for the expert, but in the majority of cases the Clergyman must be, like the one Doctor in a village, an all-round man. There is nothing more calculated to make him a man of this description than the experience which he can gain by visiting the homes of the people. This is his duty, both as a Deacon and as a Priest. As a Deacon, however, his work seems to be that of collecting information rather than that of exercising the pastoral office. The Ordinal says, " It is his office, where provision is so made, to search for the sick, poor, and impotent people of the parish, to intimate their estates, names and places where they dwell unto the Curate, that by his exhortation they may be relieved with the alms of the Parishioners and others." As a Priest he is exhorted (again in the words of the Ordinal) " to seek for Christ's sheep that are dispersed abroad, and for His children who are in the midst of this naughty world, that they may be saved through Christ for ever." The visitation of his people will increase enormously the influence of the Minister, by the knowledge which he will gain of their lives and sympathies, their trials and besetments. No method of Church work is more successful in winning men for Christ than that of the Apostles when they "went from house to house." But a distinction has to be drawn between the visits paid to the "ninety-nine" within the fold, and those to the "one astray."

I. A Visit to Every Home.

It is not advisable that in the visitation of a street, the Minister should pass from number two to four, four to six, and so on. This is too much like the method of a rent collector or a canvasser for a sewing machine. It is better to take on one afternoon Nos. 11, 30, 45, 56, 113, 248, and the next afternoon Nos. 10, 19, 36, 53, and so on. This makes a break for the visitor and causes the visit to the person concerned to be more individual and personal. A great deal of the importance of the visit is lost by Mr. A. going out of one gate only to enter the next. The course here suggested will allow every house in the street to be visited, and the visit will be far more welcome and more beneficial than if one of a series paid from door to door.

Whatever the method, the visit will require tact, resource, and above all prayer. In no branch of ministerial work is there greater need for prayer than in house to house visitation. When we knock at the door, we little know what lies behind it. There may be within that house the darkness of infidelity, the atmosphere of sin, a broken heart, or some life soured by the treachery and betrayal of some professing Christian. Surely, as we realize this, we shall remember the words of St. James, "If any man lack wisdom, let him ask of God, Who giveth to all men liberally," and as we raise the knocker with our hand, the prayer will rise from the heart, " Lord, what wilt Thou have me to do ? " If visiting is done in this spirit, then it pays, and will pay in the highest and best sense of the term, but if not, the visiting, though done, will never really have begun.

Many important points should be remembered. Courtesy is as essential when visiting in the worst slum, as when visiting in Mayfair. A knock must be given and an invitation received before entering a house. It is well, when the door is opened, to ask whether it is convenient to see the man of the house ; but when in response to our request he comes to the door, he ought not to feel that he has been called from his tea, his pipe, or his leisure for nothing. If a Flower Show or a Poultry Show is near, a subject for conversation is ready to hand, and if not, the Men's Club will serve as the purpose of the visit, *but only as an introduction*. The visitor must be prepared for any kind of reception, and whatever it is, good temper and good humour must be preserved. To lose either is fatal. A most careful watch must be kept for any opening such as : " Oh ! you were born in the country, were you ? " then probably the man will open out. Follow up, if possible, with another question—" When you were a boy, were you brought up to Church or Chapel ? " and so on. So much for a doorstep call : and even this, when carefully managed, can frequently be made to yield real spiritual fruit.

The aim of the Clergyman must always be to get inside the house. If this is accomplished, what then ? Are we simply to ask questions ? Some few years ago the West End was possessed of a craze for " slumming," and one result was that grand ladies would take a " slum " child from the East or South of London, to live for a week or so amid all the comfort and luxury of the rich. The only result was, that the child returned to the life of squalor and poverty far less contented than before. Punch seized hold of the situation, and gave us a picture of such a child sitting in a fashionable Drawing Room opposite a " Society leader." " And," said the child, " does your husband drink ? " " Of course he does not." A pause. " What wages does he earn, and how much does he give you, Mum ? " " Whatever do you mean by asking such questions, child ? " The poor child, seeing she had done wrong, sobbed out, " Mother said, when I came, I must behave as a lady, and the ladies who calls on us always asks us those questions." Such, however, is not the aim of pastoral visitation. Neither is it simply to get men and women to church, helpful as this may be.

On being invited to enter any house, the Clergyman should remove his hat, even if the man is half drunk, for he is a man, and he is in his " castle," even if it is an attic, and dirty and untidy. As the house is entered the visitor may say to himself, as Sir Oliver Lodge said concerning his work, " I am here to help God." How ? Is a child sick ? There is the opportunity. On the statue erected to the memory of Bishop Fraser, so wonderfully beloved in Manchester, is written the secret of his success. " He won all hearts by opening to them his own." Open your heart, and then what father, what mother would refuse the request ? " I am sorry ! Shall we just ask the Good Father to give the little one a good night's rest ? " This would be seizing the opportunity. Again, if a young man or a young woman is at home, questions may be asked with a cheery voice, such as " Do you play cricket ? " or " What do you do at night after business ? " " Could your mother spare you to look in at the Club one night ? " and so on. " What can I talk about ? " said a Deacon to me. If there are " sermons in stones," there are topics of conversation all around in every home. The visitor may arrive just at tea-time, and the table may be untidy, the cloth may be dirty, the bread thick, the butter " margarine," and the tea may have cost only a shilling a pound, but if asked to join in the meal, the man of God, anxious about his work and keen to win souls, will not have eyes to see these things. He will see the Christ emptying Himself for these people, and by their side he will sit, and perchance, as at Emmaus, the Saviour will be seen in the midst. To leave behind a word of Christ, a vision of Christ, is the object of all visiting. Whatever else may be gained, the absence of this result will mark the visit as a failure.

(*a*) *Public Houses must not be considered under a ban.*—They are in the parish, and the publican, his wife and children, are parishioners. I have always found publicans ready to receive visits if courtesy is shown to them, and yet frequently they feel a certain reluctance to connect themselves with anything belonging to the Church on account of their calling. An extract from a letter recently received from a publican in my parish, whose wife I had buried, shows at once the hesitation and the desire to help. " As a small but more practical proof of my gratitude, and also in memory of my dear wife, may I become an annual subscriber to one of your benevolent funds. I enclose a cheque for one guinea, which *despite your natural antipathy to the trade with which I am connected*, I hope your broadness of mind will permit you to accept, if only for the benefit of some unfortunate fellow creature." These men must be made to feel that they are not outcasts, but are welcomed most warmly in our midst.

(b) *The Pastoral Visitor must be ready for Anything.*— Some years ago, I had tried hard to win over a woman who always received me in a kindly way. She promised over and over again to come to church. One day I called in the afternoon and she promised to come to the Mission that night. I had my doubts as to whether she really meant to come, and so about three quarters of an hour before the service I called again. " Oh," she said, " I am sorry. I can't come. I've just had that basket of clothes sent in, and they must be mangled to-night." I quietly said, " You go and get ready, and I will do the mangling." She looked at me in amazement and demurred, but I stood my ground, and at last she reluctantly went, and I mangled. How I did it, and what the people said when the clothes were returned, I never inquired, but the woman that night was touched at the Mission Service by the Saviour, and I never had to go after her again. Her conversion was worth the mangling.

Another instance before leaving the subject. I visited a woman whom I knew to be living anything but a Christian life, but who was always " self-right-eous." I found her in the kitchen amid the washing tubs. After a little conversation she said, " Oh yes, I was converted twenty years ago down at Manchester." Before I visited this woman I had prayed for guidance, and quickly it came. I said to her, " I am surprised to see you washing, for you washed these very clothes only a month ago." She laughed, and looked at me and said, " Well, if I didn't keep washing them, they would soon not be fit to wear." At once I turned on

F

her, " Then what must your heart be like if it is twenty years since it was washed ? " She stopped her washing, we talked, we knelt down by the side of the tubs, and there, that afternoon, the cry went up, " God be merciful to me, a sinner," and the Angels rejoiced as the one astray got back to Him " Who cleanseth from all sin."

Souls can be saved in the home, and the visitation that pays is that which brings the Christ into the heart and life. But, what is to be done with the house where the door is closed ? Remember that after His resurrection the Lord entered the room, " the doors being shut," and that He possesses the same power to-day. Pray ye Him to enter in. Take Him in by prayer, even as Simon took Him to his mother-in-law's sickbed. No door can keep Him out, and if He gets in, the door will soon be opened for His Servant.

Empty houses should be watched, and the pastoral call should speedily follow the arrival of the new tenants.

How many hours a day should be spent in visiting ? It is a difficult question to decide, as the work in different parishes varies so much, but, if a parish is to be visited as it ought to be, at least three hours daily should be the rule. As to the length of each visit, circumstances must guide, but it is never wise to waste time in mere conversation.

Every Minister should keep a diary, not merely that he may have a register of the people visited, but for the purpose of self-examination every night. " Is this all I have done to-day ? " " Did I fail in that house ? " " Was that visit a mere social call, which might have been paid by the lawyer, or the grocer ? " These questions may tear one's heart, but it was the bleeding heart of Christ which saved the World. Each night, too, the Diary will recall to us the man in sin, the woman in sorrow, the girl in danger, and as we kneel before Him, the Chief Shepherd, we, the under Shepherds, will ask His help on behalf of these His Sheep.

II. The Visitation of Members of the Congregation.

Pastoral visitation is not confined to that of seeking the lost and the strayed. In the twenty-third Psalm we have a picture of the Good Shepherd in the midst of the Flock, and in a lesser sense this may serve as our " Ideal " concerning work amid the Flock. We are to lead them into " green pastures," and " beside still waters " ; we are to prepare a table before them, but we are to do this not merely from the Pulpit and at the Holy Table, but also in their own homes.

Clergy are beset in every parish by the temptation to visit over and over again the nice people, the people who give a warm welcome, and whom to visit is a pleasure. But this is not fulfilling the task entrusted to us.

Every Communicant, whether agreeable or disagreeable, whether living in a comfortable home, or in one room, has a claim upon the Minister. And in order to avoid being unfair, even unintentionally, in our visiting a careful register should be kept in which should be entered the date of the visit, and any special circumstances which it may be well to remember. The true parish priest will not only *see* his people in church, but *know* them in their homes. How well St. Paul knew the Communicants of his day is apparent from his Epistles, and the example displayed in the sixteenth chapter of Romans, of such intimate knowledge of men and women, is one which it is not easy for clergy to follow in their parishes. But St. Paul's interest in people was quickened by his intercession on their behalf, and if a clergyman would become interested in and keen about people, as St. Paul was, he must learn to pray for them individually. Every Communicant should be brought before God by name, and then the visit, following prayer, will not, cannot, end in a mere social call. " What did he come for ? " said a boy to his father, as a Curate left the house after a call in which he had never named the Church, her work, or the Name of the God Who had sent him. What had he come for ? An answer must be given concerning every visit.

In all congregations difficulties occasionally arise concerning some matter which the clergyman is apt to regard as so small and trivial that he treats it lightly, when, to his surprise, he finds that people are staying away from church on account of it. In a poor parish the reason for this is frequently owing to the fact that the people concerned lead narrow circumscribed lives, and that their interests are so very few. Could we express their great life interests numerically, say at six, it becomes manifest that if one interest or one sixth of all their life is touched, the effect is much more serious than if that interest were only one in a hundred or more, as is probably the case with the manifold life of the Vicar. The realization of this fact will cause the Clergy not to under-estimate the importance of matters, which at first sight may scarcely seem worthy of attention at all. Here, knowledge of his people, obtained while visiting them, is most helpful. People are more ready to listen to the man, whom they know out of the pulpit, than they are to follow one whom they know as the preacher only. The influence of the visit of a true ambassador of Christ cannot be over-estimated. He will have a message for each and for all. He will have preached on Family Prayer, and therefore when he visits he will be expected to pray. If any member of the household holds any office in the Church, whether as Churchwarden, Sunday School Teacher, or Visitor, the Minister will make inquiries with regard to the progress of such work, and will specially mention it in his prayer. When he leaves the house, every one within it, master, mistress, children, servants, will realize that a man of God has been under their roof. The atmosphere will be charged with the spiritual sense, for a Blessing has descended upon them, in answer to his cry. Happy people who have such a pastor ! for unity and power will prevail in their midst, and men will be converted and gathered within the fold of Christ.

III. The Sick, the Afflicted, the Dying.

No clergyman worthy of the name would ever refuse to visit any of his flock owing to the nature of their illness or from fear of infection. It is right, however, that he should use all reasonable precautions, not merely for his own sake, but also for the sake of his family, and of the people whom he may subsequently visit. A call upon a friendly doctor, at the commencement of his ministerial career, asking for his advice as to methods to be adopted when visiting infectious cases, will provide the candidate with the necessary information he will require.

Visits often have to be paid to the sick in Public Institutions. These usually provide a Chaplain, but even so a visit from their own Clergyman is eagerly looked forward to by the patients, and it is frequently of great value. A letter to the chaplain giving a brief account of the person's connection with the Church will be of service to him in dealing with the case, and also will tend to prevent any misunderstanding arising from his own visits to the Institution.

The larger proportion of visits to the sick will be paid to them in their own homes. If it is a chronic case, once a week will be sufficient, particularly if, as it ought to be, the visit is supplemented by visits from a member of the C.E.M.S. or some other communicant of the Church.

It is generally acknowledged among all classes of Churchmen that, as Canon Stuckey Coles, late of Pusey House, says, the Office for the Visitation of the Sick is not suitable for full use at the present time. Yet it is well worthy of study and consideration, on account of its suggestiveness, and also because certain parts of it may still well be used. The visit to the sick should be with the avowed object of causing greater peace and comfort to flow to the heart and soul, through the sufferer being brought into closer touch with Christ. This must be kept in view throughout the visit. The presence of relations and friends in the sick-room is sometimes of assistance, especially on the occasion of a first visit. The sick one is apt to be less nervous and the Visitor to be perhaps a little more general in his words, in his reading, and in his prayers. In subsequent visits, however, it is well for the Clergyman to try and get alone with the patient. This can be managed by a little tact, and by a hint given to the friends downstairs.

In dealing with the sick, the true Pastor is at once faithful, tender, and tactful. Is the person converted ? Is he at peace with God ? He is to be moved to make his position clear, and then the medicine of God's Word is to be applied. Passages of Holy Scripture suitable for various occasions should be in the mind of every visitor. The Gospel of St. John is full of helpful passages, such as the third, tenth, and fourteenth chapters. The Psalms are never out of place in the sick-room. For the Prodigal St. Luke xv. 11-32 should be read. Again such verses as the "Comfortable Words," "Him that cometh" (St. John vi. 37), "The Lord is my Shepherd" (Ps. xxiii.), "Fear thou not" (Isa. xli. 10), "If we confess our sins" (1 St. John i. 9), "He was wounded for our transgressions" (Isa. liii. 5), should never be overlooked. Hymns are of inestimable value in the sick-room, and many a weary one has found rest and joy in the Lord, as he has heard lovingly quoted : "Rock of ages"; "Just as I am"; "Jesus, Lover of my soul"; "I heard the voice of Jesus say." On the bed of sickness the life of sin can be laid at the foot of the Cross, and there hearts can become truly penitent, either rising to live out in health the life of Christ, or passing to be with Him in Paradise. A Collect, of course, can be used, but by the sick-bed, and among those whose hearts are sad, it is best to offer extempore prayer. In such a prayer blessing can be invoked on the doctor, the nurse, the patient, and on those who live in the house.

A parish priest must never forget a promise to call again. To leave such a promise unfulfilled is almost unforgivable. The visit to the bereaved is one full of difficulty. A wife is lying dead, and the husband will not be comforted. The cradle is empty, and the mother's heart is well-nigh broken. The breadwinner has passed away, and wife and children have now to face the world with all its strife and competition. At such a time, only the visit of one who has caught something of the Saviour's sympathy can be of any real help. In the poorer districts, the request will certainly be made that the body should be viewed. From this a stranger will naturally shrink, and yet to refuse will cast a slight upon the dead in the eyes of the relatives. It will be found that by doing as desired the clergyman can get frequently into closer touch with the people concerned, and that during a prayer by the side of the dead, men and women may begin to live. Visits of this nature should not be prolonged, but should be full of sympathy, hope, and faith.

IV.   **Visitation for** (a) **Private Baptism, and** (b) **Communion of the Sick.**

(a) *Private Baptism.*—In case of necessity our Church recognizes the validity of Holy Baptism in the Name of the Trinity by whomsoever it is administered, whether by mother, nurse, or servant. Usually in the event of the serious illness of an unbaptized child a clergyman is sent for. It is advisable that he should be acquainted with the rubrics connected with " Private Baptism," and if time permit, he should briefly explain the service to the mother, and to any others who may be present, and should exhort them, as the Prayer Book directs, to bring the child, if it live, to the church for its public reception. After performing the sacred rite, it is well to pray for the child and mother. Everything should be done to impress upon the minds of all present the importance of the Service. I have never been able to understand the position of clergy who, whilst they would not celebrate the Holy Communion unless they possess a private set of vessels, are yet content to administer the Sacrament of Baptism with a cup or a basin. A small Font for the purpose can be obtained. Mine was carved and presented to me by a Wesleyan when I left my last parish. It is a small matter, but one which helps to preserve that dignity which ought to be maintained, even if the Sacrament is administered in an attic.

(b) *Communion of the Sick.*—The Prayer Book does

not provide for any " Reservation of the Sacrament "
for the sick, but it does provide for a Celebration in the
sick-room. Therefore it is incumbent upon the Priest
to do everything in his power to give the sick that
which they desire, and in the manner which the Church
directs. There may be difficulties. The priest may
himself have communicated earlier in the day,
but, as the late Head of Pusey House points out in
his *Work in Country Parishes*, Bishops of the early
Church frequently celebrated several times a day.
No opinions of the priest, as to fasting or any other
question, can outweigh his obligation to administer the
Holy Communion to the sick and the dying at any hour
of the day or night. It is argued that the sick-room
may not be a fit place in which to consecrate. My
reply is that anything that makes a room unfit for the
Consecration, makes it equally unfit for the administration of the " Reserved " elements. Let us remember that the Lord, Whose Service it is, was born in a
stable, laid in a manger, and died upon a cross, and no
room can be too squalid or poverty-stricken for Him
to give Himself to the hungry souls of men, in their
hour of need. As one who has worked for many years
in a poor district, I should like to bear my testimony
to the unfailing readiness, even among the roughest of
the rough, of relatives, friends, and neighbours, to do
all in their power to make things " decent " for the
clergyman at a time of sickness. A table will be
washed, quiet on the stairs will be preserved, neighbours will take the children away, and if the clergyman
will wear his surplice, provide a white linen cloth, and
take with him his own " Communion set " and other
accessories, there is no reason why the Service should
not be conducted in a " slum " room, as reverently as in

a Cathedral. Dignity and simplicity *can* go together.

The prayer of " Humble Access," and of " Consecration" cannot be omitted without serious loss to the value of the Service. It is not for us to discuss the doctrinal questions concerning Reservation for the sick, or the reasons why the Reformers refused to allow what in Primitive days were permitted, but it is ours to carry out loyally the Prayer Book directions, and to communicate the sick in the manner prescribed. At the great Festivals, and at Easter especially, arrangements should be made whereby all the sick, infirm, and aged Communicants, who are unable to attend church, should receive the Communion in their own homes. In an understaffed parish, this perhaps can be arranged only during the Octave, but where possible, it is better to do so on the day itself. For an aged Christian, accustomed say for fifty years to the joy of Easter Communion, to pass through the day without it is no light trial. It is a privation which he should not be allowed to bear if it can be avoided. To the sick the Communion Service means much, how much only those who have gone through sickness without it really know, and the efficient parish priest will put its administration as a duty never to be neglected or overlooked.

V. In The Open Air.

In recent years the Church has realized the folly of leaving unoccupied so magnificent a field for successful work as that which is afforded in the Open Air. The " march " on Good Friday, 1911, through London of that great procession organized by the Bishop of London's Evangelistic Council, and the Open Air Services in Hyde Park and elsewhere, conducted under the same auspices, testify to the aroused interest in this work on the part of the Church. One condition must be laid down concerning all work in the open air. It must be worthy of the Church which it represents, and must be of the very best possible character. How much harm has been done to the Church of Christ by the number of feeble and inefficient services in the open air will never be known. Frankly, if I were a man of the world, and passed *some* " Open Air " Services and heard *some* speakers, I think I should thank God that I never went to church if that was the kind of preaching given there. If a Church has two preachers, the one inferior and the other good, my suggestion is that the former should be put up inside where the people have prayed for patience and are supposed to possess it, and that the good speaker should be reserved for the outside, where he is needed more. This does not imply that laymen should be excluded from the Open Air platform. In many instances they are able to produce an impression far greater than that produced by the ordinary clergyman. They should be encouraged in this work, and if possible guided as to the best methods to be followed. Think of the congregation which the Open Air speaker may have : here an infidel ; there a jailbird ; close by a woman who has lost her faith amid the sorrows of life ; behind her one who was formerly a Churchwarden, and how great was his fall. Surely for these the Church should give her best, for it was for such that the Good Shepherd gave His Life.

The site of the Service will depend upon the locality, but the quiet of a side street is preferable to the noise of a main thoroughfare. The speaker should stand with his back to the wind, and if he can face a wall or a building, with sufficient space for the crowd in between, he will speak the more easily and be the better heard, especially if he is raised on a suitable platform. Such a platform can easily be made and should be portable. The question of a lamp is not an easy one to decide. Its use certainly enables the reading of hymns, but it is also apt to cause hesitation in the minds of some, who, if it were dark, would mingle with the crowd. On the whole I think a lamp should be used if the crowd is a large one, for then the number gathered round will give the passer-by some confidence in joining them, but for a small crowd it is better not to have a lamp, or, if one at all, one which does not give a bright light.

The music is important. The hymns should be carefully selected from those which are generally known. What memories are stirred by the singing of " Rock of Ages," or of " Jesus, Lover of my soul." If the conductor in announcing the hymn can narrate some incident connected with its authorship or history, he will quicken the interest of the crowd and make the singing more real. " Nearer, my God, to Thee " will for all time have an added power by its association with the loss of the *Titanic*. A harmonium is more useful than a cornet, and tends to keep the singing together in tune and time—no easy task in the open air. At the largest services in my parish hymn-books are handed round. The percentage of missing or strayed books is very small, and this is recompensed by the hope that they may become tracts in the homes to which they have been carried.

But what of the address ? Bishop Thorold laid down four points at which the speaker should aim :—

1st. To be listened to, therefore he should be interesting.

2nd. To be understood, therefore he should be clear.

3rd. To be useful, therefore he should be practical.

4th. To be obeyed, therefore he should speak as the Oracle of God.

The Speaker must decide whether his address is to be mainly evidential or evangelistic. If he takes the former line in districts like East or South of London, it is almost certain that he will be interrupted by questioners. If he is wise he will take them with good temper and answer the questions seriously. I have known an interruption to cause a meeting to become all at once " alive." The speaker obtains an opportunity and a hearing which he would not otherwise have had.

Whether indoors or in the street, the preacher has only one message, and that is Christ. Christ, not merely as Social Reformer, but as the eternal Son of God, Who loved men and gave Himself for men, the Saviour of the World. Results from such preaching are bound to ensue. Wesley said that the result of his three days' preaching, standing upon his father's tombstone, were greater than those that followed his three years' sermons in his father's pulpit. Recently a friend of mine told me that three persons quite unknown to each other came forward for Confirmation as the result of the same address at the same Open Air Service. It is well to have two or three discreet workers in the crowd who *have eyes to see*, and who can quietly move about, and if a chance presents itself to get into conversation with persons on the outskirts of the crowd. A pledge book should be in readiness, not that it is wise to attempt to obtain signatures publicly ; but a pledge can be torn out and given to a man or woman to sign at home. Names of persons can also be obtained with a view to visits being paid to them in their homes. Invitations can be given to special services for men or for women, or to the Sunday Evening Services. In the Open Air, three or four short telling addresses are far preferable to one or two long ones.

One word must be added—the first Open Air Service resulted not merely in the conversion of three thousand persons, but in their Baptism as well. Efforts should be made to link the Open Air work with definite Church life, a result frequently overlooked. The speakers and all the helpers should see that the whole service is reverent throughout. To see workers talking and laughing while a brother is speaking is not calculated to impress the passer-by with regard to the seriousness of the message given. What produced such a mighty result at Jerusalem ? Surely it was not solely the sermon of St. Peter, which after all was but a summary of our Lord's Life and Death. Is not the secret to be discovered in the fact that the preacher was " filled with the Holy Ghost," and that he was surrounded by one hundred and twenty men and women who for ten days had prayed themselves into one accord and who had received the " Baptism of Power." The fact that three thousand were converted is explained by the power which these men of Israel had with God and with men, and that was the reason why they prevailed. Our aim must be to take into the street for the service the whole congregation—Wardens and Sidesmen, as well as the humbler folk—all filled with the Spirit, and then signs and wonders will be wrought in His Name.

VI. Parochial Missions.

It is becoming more and more difficult to arouse keen interest in a " Mission." In years gone by, the holding of a Mission was an event which stirred Churchmen and Nonconformists on the one side, and the careless and the profane on the other.

That day has largely gone. Various reasons may

be given for this change. Missions are not now new.
The Salvation Army has made all such special efforts
common and ordinary. Again, in some districts, the
moment a Vicar perceived any falling off in his congregation, a Mission was proposed, and frequently rushed
through without adequate thought, prayer or preparation. Thus many people became familiar with the
name and method of a Mission without receiving the
blessing which ought to follow from it. Yet Parochial
Missions have their distinct place in the life of a parish.
They should not be held too frequently. Five years at
least should elapse between them. The preparation
should be very real. The Church should be gathered
for prayer, plans of work drawn up, tasks assigned, a
special choir formed, houses visited, and an open air
campaign arranged. Into this work all the Clergy
should throw themselves heartily. They may be
tempted to do otherwise, for perhaps the Missioner,
whoever he may be, may adopt some methods which
may not only not appeal to the minister personally, but
even jar upon him ; but in the midst of a Mission the
Priest must be as the soldier in the midst of the battle,
loyal through and through, obeying even if a command appears as unwise as that which led to disaster
at Balaclava. The Church at Ephesus was born in
excitement, and if sin is sin, and hell is hell, and if the
Cross is stained with the Life-Blood of our Lord, then
it will be little wonder if the Missioner who realizes
these things, does depart from ordinary methods and
bends all his powers to call some sinners to repentance
and to a new life in God.

VII. **Extra Services and Meetings.**

Services of a different nature are frequently held with
a view to bringing in the outsider. If these are held in

church, permission must previously be obtained from the Bishop. In subsequent lectures I hope to deal with special services for men and women, but here it may be well to consider the best methods for successfully conducting some of those services which are being blessed to-day in many parishes.

(a) *Lantern Services.*—These should not be held too frequently, or the novelty will wear off, and the pictures will become stale. A series of such services can well be arranged during Lent or Advent after the Evening Service. In some churches, at such services, the lights are never turned up, so that the poorest of the poor may attend, just as they are, without feeling shame at any one seeing their clothes.

With regard to such services care must be taken :—

1st. That reverence is maintained throughout. A Lantern Service without reverence becomes like a show in a Picture Palace, and therefore it is important that everything should be conducted in such a manner as to impress the fact upon all present that it is still a service in church.

2nd. That the slides are of good quality, and that the addresses are carefully prepared.

The lantern must be a good one, and of sufficient power : the operator must be a man in full sympathy with the object of the service, and one who understands his work. If the conductor of the service requires notes, it will add to his comfort if he has a dark lantern in the pulpit. An electric cord should be fixed so as to connect him with the operator, in order that the change of slides may work smoothly. *The slides must be of the very best quality*. Many so-called sacred pictures ought never to be exhibited in any building connected with the Church. Slides which are crude, inartistic, and almost bordering upon the indecent, should be carefully avoided. After several years' experience I can strongly recommend those of Messrs. Newton & Co., 37, King Street, Covent Garden. They represent the finest sacred pictures of all ages, and are to be depended upon for beauty of design, colour, and execution. For services during Lent, Holy Week, and especially on Good Friday, they are most appropriate, and if the lectures issued with them compiled by the Rev. G. R. Balleine and others are studied, the parish priest will have no reason to regret the holding of Lantern Services during these special seasons of the Church's Year.

(b) *Midnight Services.*—These may be of two kinds.

1st. That which is commonly called a " Watchnight Service," which is held on the last night of the old year. Objections are raised to such services on the ground that they are sensational, and that numbers come to them who are never found in the church at other times. With regard to the first objection, it may be said that if such a service is *merely* sensational, the blame must be borne solely by the Clergy in charge. They *can* be made just what the Clergy desire.

The first year I held this service at Bethnal Green, men actually spat over the side gallery into the body of the church, but to-day the people in the galleries are as reverent as could be desired, though year by year the church is packed to overflowing with just the same kind of people as at first. A second objection is raised that many people who come attend no other service throughout the year. Concerning large numbers of those attending this charge is probably correct, but this is a reason for, rather than against, such services being held. The real justification for this service lies in the fact that many of the people find the Midnight Service the beginning, not only of a New Year, but also of a New Life. The service ought to be of a purely mission character—simple, hearty, congregational, and evangelistic in the best meaning of the term. The doors should be closed during the prayers and the address, so that quietness may be the better preserved, and the whole congregation should kneel in silent prayer as they are leaving the old and entering into the New Year. In my own church I announce the Motto for the New Year, and invite every one to come to church on the next Sunday night when it will be taken as the text. As the congregation leave the church a sealed envelope is handed to each person. It contains a specially printed pledge card, and also one containing a renewal of dedication to God. These are not intended to be returned to the Vicar, but are for private signature when alone with God. I have evidence that these silent messages have led to many persons making the " great decision " and of henceforth seeking to live the New Life.

2nd. The other kind of " Midnight Service " is one held expressly to deal with frequenters of public-houses. These services are better held in some hall than in church. They should commence immediately the public-houses are closed. A small band of workers should be told off to lie in wait outside each public-house with a card of invitation, and with instructions to try to bring the people with them. It is advisable that a cup of coffee and a bun should be provided. Time will thus be given for stragglers to come in and for the " mixed " company to get accustomed to their surroundings before the meeting begins. The meeting should be quite unconventional, extempore prayer should be offered, and the address should not be so much a denunciation of Drink and its evils (although this cannot be overlooked altogether) as a direct appeal to the highest and best in man. A spirit of hopefulness should characterize it from beginning to end, that even the most hopeless person may be led to think—" There is hope for me," and also to say : " I will arise and go to my Father." Pledges should be taken, but above all the Gospel message must be preached and received or the Pledge will mean little. A gathering such as this must be followed by a visit to all who seem in any way to have been influenced. People of such a character have a far more difficult battle to fight than we imagine, and they must receive the most sympathetic and watchful consideration, and be picked up just as often as they fall.

(c) *Cottage Meetings.*—In working-class and slum parishes, Cottage Meetings may be introduced with great advantage so long as they are worked as stepping-stones to, and not as substitutes for, the Church Services. They should not be allowed to degenerate into mere gatherings of the few Christians in the Street, or into a second edition of a Mothers' Meeting. If these dangers are guarded against, such meetings may become useful adjuncts of other parochial agencies.

(d) *Meetings in General.*—In well-organized parishes meetings on behalf of all kinds of societies will be held. If such are to be really successful, the following points should be observed :—

1. They should commence punctually and not be unduly prolonged.

2. The Chairman should be a man who can preside without monopolizing the whole time of the Meeting.

3. The Speakers should not be too numerous, and

each should be enjoined to leave time for his brethren
to do more than merely catch the last train.

4. Votes of thanks should be excluded, excepting
upon rare and very special occasions. They are not
always advisable, and they frequently mar any good
impression previously produced by the meetings.

VIII. Amusements—Clubs—Social Work.

(a) *Amusements*.—Dr. Griffith Thomas says that
the Mission of the Church is :—

1. To witness for Christ.
2. To win souls.
3. To set Christians to work.
4. To watch over and feed her individual members.

If this is correct, then amusements will seem to be
outside her scope in parochial work. Christianity
cannot be divorced from any side of a person's life.
Every part of life should be brought under the sway
of Christ the King. If that is so, the Church is bound
to have a message to give concerning the amusements
of the people which, frequently, are to the tired and
weary worker a real recreation and refreshment. Care
must be taken—

1. That nothing is countenanced which is inconsistent with the mission of the Church.

2. That all amusements are in reality, as well as in
name, merely small adjuncts of the Church's work.
They must not become too prominent, nor take up too
much time or thought.

3. That they do not become substitutes for the
" freewill offerings " of the people, or in other words,
an easy and agreeable way of raising funds for the work
of the Church. To do so is to degrade the " offerings
to the Lord " until they become a mere payment for
an hour's amusement.

Within these limits, Open Air Fêtes, Social Gatherings, and other Entertainments can be held at intervals. The programme should be strictly examined beforehand, and encores carefully watched, because an excellent programme may be spoiled by an undesirable item introduced as an encore.

(b) *Clubs.*—These will be discussed more fully when we consider Men's Work, but Sir Robertson Nicoll's saying may be well remembered : " That a Church may have a Soup Kitchen, but the Church must take care lest it is itself turned into a Soup Kitchen." Clubs must not occupy too prominent a position in the work of the Church, and should never be without a connecting link with it.

(c) *Social Work.*—" Godliness is profitable for the life that now is." Our Lord's teaching is full of reference to social work, and in the view which He presents of the " Final Judgment " men are seen to be judged according to their recognition or rejection of what, to-day, are termed " social " duties. The proceedings of the Last Lambeth Conference reveal how far the Church is beginning to realize her duty in this respect. On such subjects she can, as the Conference points out, work in co-operation with Nonconformists, and so in matters relating to Intemperance, Impurity, and Gambling, she must, together with all Christian people, wage unceasing war. Parochially much can be done, by the suppression of immoral houses, by care lest laws relating to the public-houses are not faithfully administered, and by an active share in the work of the local Board of Guardians. Other spheres of social work are open both to clergy and laity. A Medical Mission, even in these days of the National Insurance Act, has a distinct place in parochial life, for it enables

the medical men frequently to convey a hint to the
clergy that in one case food is more necessary than
drugs, and in another a young girl has " gone wrong,"
or again, that a young fellow is fast going into
consumption through his own acts.   In many ways a
Medical Mission can render help of the greatest benefit,
not only to the physical, but also to the moral and
spiritual life of men.

In a working-class parish, a Lodging House, or, as
it is more commonly called, a " Working Men's Hotel,"
can afford excellent accommodation at a cheap rate
for the single men of the labouring and coster class.

With regard to the Relief of the Poor, the Church has
a duty to perform.   The difficulties in connection with
this are so great, and abuses are so difficult to avoid,
that many people have advocated that the Church's
policy should be to let the question alone, and leave it
to the Boards of Guardians and other bodies, such as
the C.O.S., to deal with. I confess that I have " not so
learned Christ " or my New Testament.   With the
example of Christ and of the Apostles before us, I am
compelled to recognize that the Church must care for,
and relieve, the destitute and the sick, irrespective of
race or creed.   Lecky tells us that it was "Christianity which first made Charity a rudimentary virtue,"
and the Church must not cease to regard it as such.
Great care must be exercised that all that is done will
tend to build up, rather than to undermine, responsibility.   It is better in some cases to administer relief
in kind, by means of tickets on various tradespeople,
than by a gift of money.   Suitable families should be
assisted to emigrate, and co-operation should be sought
with the local " Care Committees " which deal with
the employment of children on their leaving School.

In many ways too numerous to mention the Church should be to the fore in the administration of practical Social Reform.

In connection with this subject I strongly recommend that for some months between their University course and their Ordination, men who seek Holy Orders should reside in some Settlement, where they may become acquainted on the spot with the inner life of the people, and also the better study the best methods of Social Reform. Oxford House, Ridley House (the Settlement connected with my parish), both in Bethnal Green ; Cambridge House, the Oxford and Cambridge Medical Missions, all in South London, and other similar institutions, are always available for Ordinands, and particulars as to residence can be obtained from their respective Wardens.

In all these varied ways the Church must be alive to her duty in fighting for her Lord outside the Building called by her name. She must be in action : she must not slumber : in every part of the parish she must make her influence felt. By visitation she must invade the homes of the people and capture them for her Lord, or in them give comfort, help, and guidance to His children. In the Open Air, and by means of Parochial Missions, Lantern and Midnight Services, she must supplement the ordinary methods of her work, if by any means she can save some. By her guidance in the recreative side of life, and by her teaching and help amid all the social problems of the age, she must convince the world that in everything Christianity takes its side on behalf of right, and that the Lord rules over the bodies as well as over the souls of men. In the Parish the Cross must be uplifted and men taught to look at Him Who died that they may begin to live.

LECTURE THE FOURTH

In Reaching Men

THE urgent necessity for aggressive work among men is admitted on all hands. In this Lecture it is impossible to deal adequately with this question,[1] but there are several points which can be raised.

I. Men are not Reached.

This is evident in all parts of the country. Even in churches where in the congregation a fair proportion of men are to be found, the total number present will be exceedingly small in comparison with the population. The following figures relating to the proportion of communicants in the Church of England to the population afford much food for consideration. The Diocese of Hereford easily occupies the first place with fourteen per cent., while Durham is the lowest with only four per cent. London and Manchester have five per cent., while Southwark is a little better with five and a half per cent. These figures are deplorable. Further be it noted that they include women as well as men ; and speaking generally, the small proportion of men to women at an ordinary Celebration is striking evidence to the truth of the assertion that the Church has failed to reach the men. In considering this question we

[1] I would refer those who desire to consider this subject more fully to *Fishers of Men* or *How to Win the Men*, 2s. net, published by Robert Scott, Paternoster Row.

must first discuss some of the reasons for this failure to
win men for Christ.

(a) *The Indifference of the Church in the Past.*—The
Church has not adapted herself to meet modern needs.
The Prayer Book Services are magnificent and spiritual ; but they are essentially services for those who
have been educated in the doctrines of the Church and
for the " ninety and nine that safely lay in the shelter of
the fold." The Church requires a revision of her
Prayer Book that will provide services essentially for
the " one astray." This the Church has not provided.
If on some Sunday night the ordinary congregation
could be induced to remain at home, and the Parish
Church could be filled with the careless, the indifferent,
the drunkards, and the profligates of our parishes, it
would be seen that Evening Prayer, as at present con-
structed, would not appeal to such a congregation.
They would not know where the psalms are, or what
was being said or sung after the lessons were read.
Again, even in visiting, the men are missed by the
Clergy, because the call is usually made in the afternoon
when only the women are at home.

(b) *The Gap which frequently Separates Clergy and
Laity in Thought and Attitude towards the Problem of
Life.*—That such a gap exists is only too apparent,
whether we turn either to the West End or to the East
End. Visit the restaurant in one of the leading hotels
on a Sunday night and see every table occupied, and if
we could pass from one to another what percentage of
those present would have been found in church that
day ? Again let us take our stand on Tower Hill, in
the midst of some great strike, and as we gaze into the
faces of the twenty or thirty thousand men gathered
there, let us ask whether that type is often seen in

church on the Lord's Day ?   Life, Philosophy, Politics,
Social Reform, together with Ecclesiastical Questions
(the latter especially), are frequently seen by laymen
from a totally different point of view from that of
the clerical mind. The Bishop of Liverpool says,
" We must guard against a Conservatism which prevents us from keeping an open mind and adapting
ourselves to changing circumstances, habits of thought,
and fresh accessions of knowledge." This can only be
accomplished by our reading being sufficiently wide for
the grasp of different views on the great subjects, which
men rank as most important, and by a frank discussion
with men on their difficulties of faith and life. The
man who presents a view other than that which might
be considered orthodox must not be made to feel that he
is an outcast in consequence ; his view must be carefully considered and his right of private judgment fully
respected.

(c) *The Social Conditions of the Present Day.*—Men
are influenced against attendance at church by—

(1) *The Position of Sunday.*—Sunday is fast becoming either a day merely of pleasure or of labour. On the
one hand, cheap excursions, concerts or kinemato-
graphs, in ever-increasing numbers, are attracting their
thousands. On the other hand, the larger this number
becomes the more work is entailed. It is stated that
already one adult in eight is at work on the Lord's Day.

(2) *The Condition of Homelife.*—Among men and
women overworked and underpaid, and living in an
overcrowded and congested area, Sunday frequently
becomes a day when they turn their attention either to
the Public-House or to the Park, or more frequently it is
spent by them in their own homes either for work, or
for rest.   Half an hour's visiting in certain districts

will reveal the fact that "Home" is practically non-existent for multitudes at the present day. A million mothers are daily engaged in manual labour of one kind or another ; over one hundred thousand children are ill-treated annually in Christian England, as the report of the Society for Prevention of Cruelty to Children shows ; over a million and a half of people in London are members of families, the total earnings of each of which is under a guinea per week. These people are apt to ask, "What is the good of Christianity?" "It does nothing for us." Living under conditions such as these, can any who come to the church for the sake of the loaves and fishes be severely blamed ? How many in other walks of life would do the same if they lived under similar conditions !

It is well to bear in mind that although appalling social conditions may and do tend to prevent attendance at church, it does not necessarily follow that if they were improved church-going would be increased. During my recent visit to Australia and New Zealand (sometimes called the "Working Man's Paradise"), I heard over and over again the assertion made that the good social conditions under which men lived were the cause of non-attendance at church. Men were too prosperous, so it was asserted, to feel the great need of religious consolation and help, and certainly the attendance at church in the West End of London does not afford any evidence that good social conditions increase either respect for Sunday or desire after God or His House. The real reason lies much deeper than environment.

(d) *Scepticism*.—Infidelity is not gaining ground so rapidly as is supposed. Agnosticism is probably increasing among the wealthier classes ; but the great majority of the working classes, while indifferent to the claims of God, declare their belief in Him. The few children withdrawn from religious instruction in Day Schools, the desire for their children to be baptized, the Churching of Mothers, the few funerals that are unaccompanied by religious rites, all afford evidence of a religious spirit even in the apparently " irreligious " classes. While it is unwise to ignore the influence of the cheap publications of the Rationalistic Press which have so largely increased during recent years, care must be taken lest an exaggerated importance be attached to them. The *Origin of Species* is said to have been sold by tens of thousands, but when it is remembered that even Huxley declared how difficult it had been for him to read it through, we can realize that there is a difference between a book bought and a book read. That the thoughtful leaders of the Working Classes are not opposed to Christianity is shown by the fact that of the forty-one Labour Members of Parliament over thirty are active workers in connection with some Christian Body or other. Still, the representatives of the Rationalistic party are active, and in the parks and elsewhere their assertions must be challenged and their arguments must be met.

While discussing this point, reference may be made to the baneful influence which the inconsistent lives of so many professing Christians exercise upon men. The tyranny of masters and foremen known to be members of some Church, equally with the lack of real principle manifested in the lives of their Christian comrades, frequently cause men to hold aloof from all Christian bodies. It is most important to recognize that this is a more powerful factor than Infidelity in the task which the Church has to accomplish, and one which can be met only by pressing home the great truth that "Faith without works" is dead and that Christian men are to be known by the manifestation of the fruits of the Spirit in their lives.

(e) *Sin.*—But the real reason for non-attendance at church is Sin—Sin of some kind or other and which alienates the soul from God. The craving for drink, the desire for wealth, impurity and gambling, are some of the grosser manifestations of Sin. Some Clergy are tempted through mistaken sentimentality to excuse men in their sin; but sin *is* always sin. It is that which has alienated men from God, it is that which has produced all the misery of the world, and that which cost Christ His Life upon the Cross. Sin must never be looked upon as a mere failing; but declared to be what it is, at once the maker of Hell and the product of Hell.

II. Men can be Reached.

(a) *If Men's Work is put First.*—The teaching of the New Testament and the practice of the Apostles alike put Men's work in the forefront of the Church's work. No other effort can come before it or supersede it without serious injury being inflicted upon the progress of Christianity. The proposition that men of forty are so fixed in their habits of thought and life that it is almost impossible for them to change, and that therefore the next generation must be saved by reaching the children of the present one, has proved itself in past days to be as contrary to fact as it is contrary to the teaching of Scripture. The adults of the present generation *are* the children of the last, who were taught the Faith in Sunday Schools and in Day Schools, yet they are to-day the "lapsed masses" who form the great problem which awaits solution. But what do the Scriptures assert ? Surely it is apparent in the New Testament that the glory of the early Church was centred in its victory over men by the power of the Holy Ghost and in the Name of Christ. Men were won here, won there, won everywhere. There was no suggestion by St. Paul at Ephesus, or elsewhere, that men were too difficult to be reached by " the Name," and that it was only children that could be influenced by It. To all the Apostles, as well as St. Paul, it was " the only Name given among men by which they must be saved," but it was all-sufficient, and men were saved. Away with such a lowering of the Gospel standard and all that is implied by the exaltation of work among children above that among men. The Church, strong in her faith in God, must go forth boldly to fight for men, and not merely for women and children. If she thus goes forth, she will gain the men, and if they are gained, and every home becomes a " Bethel," and every father a man of prayer, she will have done more for the next generation than if she had opened a Sunday School in every street. The godly home and the praying father will do far more for the conversion of the men and women of the future than any other influence ; and therefore in the interests of childlife, and in the interest of future generations, the Church must put men's work first, and not permit of any other occupying that position.

(b) *If the Power of " Personality " is not ignored.*— There is a tendency to ignore " Personality " and to lay exaggerated stress upon the Church or on a Society. " Men ought to do this because of the Church " : they ought to attend church because it is the church, no matter who the preacher may be, and so on. There is a great deal to be said in favour of such teaching because there is a large element of truth in it. But it must be remembered, that all through the ages, both before and after Christ, it pleased God to work through personality. It was a Moses, and not a Society, that led the Israelites out of bondage. It was not owing to the deliberations of a Committee that the Cross was planted in Macedonia, but through a vision which appeared to a man with a personality. What were the " Early Fathers " but men who possessed a personality ? The great movements known as the Reformation, the Evangelical Revival, the Tractarian Movement, all owed their success largely to the " Personality " of the men associated with them. Can any one think of the Reformation apart from Luther, or the Evangelical Revival without a Wesley and Whitfield, or the " Tractarian Movement " apart from Newman, Pusey, and Keble.

The power of " Personality " must be recognized as one of the most influential factors in the work of the Church, and the young Clergyman must remember that although certain men may be gifted in a peculiar manner, yet all men may cultivate " Personality " if they will. St. Paul surely had this in his mind when he wrote to Timothy (1 Tim. i. 16), " Take heed to thyself " (Personality) " and to the doctrine " (Truth). Personality does not imply imitation, for a man to be strong must be himself, and a strong personality is simply a man *at his best*. His best may lie in the direction of intellect, or of heart. Men with a personality vary, and the character of their gifts vary, but the preacher must take heed to himself, his personality. He must stir up the gift within him and play the man. Here Clergy are sometimes weak. Contrast the Labour leader as he speaks with the Minister as he preaches. Whether we agree with the former or not, we realize he is *a man*, and as such is speaking to men. Let the clergyman be a *man* and he will emerge the stronger, the *Priest of God* with power.

III. Methods of Work.

All men are not moved in the same way. Frequently men of the parish are not stirred by that which moves the Vicar, while on the other hand the parish is profoundly impressed by some influence which does not in the slightest appeal to their Minister. The fisherman who is wise baits his hook with that which will tempt the particular kind of fish he wishes to catch, and so the "Fisher of Men" does not try merely one method but many. If one method does not succeed he tries another. He does not adapt the services of the Church to suit himself but to catch men : he does not employ this method or that simply because he likes it, for he may personally resent it ; but he uses it because there may be a man whom it will bring to Christ. " He is all things to all men " that he may save some. He knows that Christ healed the man who was brought to Him through the roof by the exceptional method, and he, too, is prepared thus to bring a man to Christ if he can do so by no other way. Yet he does not nail up all the doors, or, in other words, close down all ordinary methods. He leaves such open that men may pass through them into the Presence of Christ. Thus, although he has a Men's Service or a Lantern Service, he ceases not to keep open the doors for Morning and Evening Prayer, that in these ordinary services men may know there is present " the Power " to heal them. But if he cannot bring men one way he tries another, and one such that has been blessed of God to many is that of—

IV. Men's Services.

(*a*) *The Character of such a Service.*—Men's Services

have become very common in recent years. Their usefulness cannot now be questioned, and many reasons in
their favour can be advanced. Men are not so loth to
attend a service in their working clothes if it is only for
men. Again topics can be discussed at such a service
which it would be unwise to introduce in a mixed congregation, although it is perhaps a mistake to allow the
impression to become current that only such subjects
are discussed. But if such a service is held, its relation
to the Evening Service must be clearly defined. It
must not be a copy or an imitation of it, for if it is so,
then the Evening Service might be supposed to do its
work, and thus there would be no justification for the
existence of the special one in the afternoon. On the
other hand, it must not be antagonistic to it in the
spirit, or out of harmony with it in practice. If the
Men's Service fulfils its purpose, it will not be a drag
upon the Church but that which will strengthen her
by leading men to the Evening Service and to full Communion with the Church. To achieve this end the
better it should be held in the church in preference to a
hall, that the passage to the Evening Service may be
the easier. It should be continued every Sunday and
not once a month, and it would then tend to regular
observance of the Sabbath. It will not become a P.S.A.
existing merely for the purpose of giving men a pleasant
Sunday afternoon, nor will it tend to be an entertainment or a semi-political meeting with a dash of religion
thrown in, it will be a religious service from beginning
to end, and one in which every effort will be made to
lead men to think, to repent and to turn to God through
faith in Christ.

The whole service must be hearty and congregational.
The Minister in charge must endeavour, apart from the

address, to make it of such a nature that the men, rather than he should conduct it. The music, is especially important in a service such as this. An orchestra, not professional, composed of the men themselves, will be of great value, if it is kept to its right work. It can lead the singing and can play for a quarter of an hour previous to the Service, and in addition contribute a Voluntary at the close. What Hymn-book should be used ? *The Durham Mission Hymn-book* is good ; but I much prefer what to many may seem a thoroughly unorthodox collection. I mean the enlarged " *Sankey*." I know the objections raised. " It is not a Church Hymn-book." But at present there is no such *authorized* book in existence, for Hymns *Ancient and Modern, The Hymnal Companion, Church Hymns*, and all such books are merely compilations, and are *published without authority*. While this is the position, is not the selection of any Hymn-book, American or otherwise, which best suits a particular class of people, the wisest solution for the chaotic condition, and *Sankey's*, with all its faults, is, in my opinion, the best book we have for this special purpose. We find in it many of the old hymns like " Jesu, Lover of my soul," together with a large selection of hymns of a distinctly Mission character, and these frequently with a chorus which men so delight in singing. Many men who are excellent workers in my church were led to God while singing " Where is my wandering boy to-night ? " while others found their way back to the Father while trying to answer the question, " Are you coming home to-night ? " or during the singing of " There were ninety and nine that safely lay." The singing of Solos should be carefully watched. A hymn full of an appeal to the heart is far preferable to " Arm, Arm, ye brave," and yet it is the latter kind of music which the soloist prefers.

The Prayers should not consist of a few collects said by the Priest, for if such becomes the custom it prevents men from learning at this Service, either to pray for themselves, or to become accustomed to a printed liturgy. The Prayer Book itself should not be introduced owing to its complex character, and because it does not contain any " Form " which is quite suitable for such a service ; but a special Liturgy (such as, for instance, that which we use in our own Church[1]) should be obtained, a copy handed to each man, and the page announced as the Service begins. Thus the men will begin to hear their own voice in prayer, and will commence to follow a " Service." This will pave the way for the authoritative Evening Order by and by.

The reading of the Lesson is important. Two plans may be alternately adopted with advantage. A member of the Committee can read one Sunday, while on the next the Minister should do so himself. But in this latter case he should not read it alone. Bibles should be provided for all present. For this purpose grants in aid of their purchase may be obtained from the Society for Promoting Christian Knowledge, or from the British and Foreign Bible Society. The Chapter should be announced and *also* the number of the page, so as to aid the men in finding the places, and also to prevent them from feeling awkward in not knowing where it is to be found. When every man has found the Lesson, the Minister should read one verse and the men the next. By this method men learn to handle a Bible, to open it, and to read it themselves. I have known men who

[1] *Liturgies for Men's Services.* Murray & Co., 11, Ludgate Square, E.C.

have become so much interested in a Chapter that they have read that particular Book through the same night.

As for the Address, what I have previously said upon preaching applies, with even greater force, to an address at a special gathering composed of men only. If men are to be moved, the manuscript must not be taken into the pulpit, and the message must be delivered as from man to man. The subjects must be varied. It is unadvisable to take a " course," for although this method might hold together the thoughtful men, the discussion of the same subject for several Sundays in succession would tend to cause the other men to cease attending. If a subject dealing with Christian Evidence is dealt with one week, a subject like the " Prodigal Son " should be taken the next and so on, and thus the various elements which compose the Service will be held together. Social topics must not be brought forward too prominently, and party Politics must be barred. It will be found far more profitable as a rule for one of the parochial clergy to give an address, than for a stranger with a big name to occupy the pulpit too frequently. The latter may attract larger numbers, but the former is more likely to produce a deeper and a more lasting impression. If, now and then, a Missionary can be secured, and if he can be induced to tell the " Story " of his work, he will frequently remove prejudices concerning Foreign Mission work, and will also stimulate Missionary Enterprise.

The message, whatever the subject, must be a live one—straight, manly, and direct—burning with a holy enthusiasm for Christ. If ever a preacher should be " red hot " when speaking, it should be at a Men's Service. But the " glow " must be real and not a " make up," for men can quickly discriminate between the one and the other. The Preacher who comes to point out to men " the Lamb of God " must be a " burning " as well as a " shining " light. He must be " filled with the Holy Ghost." A " John the Baptist," or a " St. Peter," are, after all, no different from other men, except that they were Spirit-filled men. This distinction makes *all the difference* between failure and success, between fruit and no fruit, between " the unfulfilled Mission " and the " Well done " of Christ.

If the Preacher wishes to ascertain what men really wish to know, he cannot do better than provide a box at the door of the church into which they can put any questions dealing with Scriptural, Evidential, or Ecclesiastical subjects. These should be edited, and compressed into a simple direct question, then published by means of poster and card, and answered at the Service once in every six weeks. This " answering " will take the place of the address. " Question Sunday " is not only interesting, but distinctly useful.

(*b*) *The Organization of such a Service.*—Thoroughly efficient organization pays at a Men's Service as elsewhere, but it must be on democratic lines. A strong committee should be formed, not necessarily entirely of C.E.M.S. men, for that would exclude men who have not seen their way to join that Society, and yet can render willing and efficient aid to a Men's Service. The committee should be elected only partly by the members at the Annual Meeting, for the Vicar should nominate either one-third, or one-half, of the whole number. This is advisable, if for no other reason than that men who really do the work might be entirely left out on a popular vote. The secretary must be carefully selected. He should be a man of enthusiasm and tact.

Inside the church efforts should be made to ensure that every man attending the Service receives a warm welcome. The church should be divided into blocks over each of which a superintendent should be appointed. The blocks should be divided again into sections of about three pews, and each section should be placed under the charge of a member of the committee, who should supply each man under his care with a Bible, Hymn-book, and Liturgy, together with a card announcing the next week's subject, which he should be asked to give to a friend. Men attending casually should be induced (but no sort of compulsion should be used) to join the Service, and on their doing so, should be given a badge, a card of membership, and a number. They should be asked to give this number to the Registrar as they may enter the church week by week, and from the number sheet the register can be marked on the Monday. At the close of the Service the Vicar, or whoever has given the address, should shake hands with each man as he leaves, and extend an invitation to old-comers to attend the Evening Service, and to new-comers to come again.

(c) *The Best Methods of " Outside " Work, i.e. Getting Men into the Service.*

(1) *By a Brass Band.*—The initial cost of a Brass Band is rather heavy, but the result obtained is worth it, providing that the Band is formed of keen men who belong to the Service. The Band should play in procession through the streets of the parish three quarters of an hour before the Service, and should be headed by a banner and accompanied by members of the committee, who should distribute cards to men in the streets, or at their doors as the Band passes along.

(2) *By Clubs.*—Clubs as a means of getting men to

church fail far more frequently than they succeed. Men can be induced by the hundred to join a club, but its atmosphere is merely that of the parts which compose it, and therefore it scarcely ever feeds or strengthens the Church. My plan has ever been, not to use the club as a means of feeding the Church, but rather to reverse the process and to get men to God and to church, and then to establish a club and so provide innocent recreation for the men so won. The club will then be in hearty sympathy with the Church and the Men's Service, and so if a man from the street joins it, in less than a month one of two things usually occurs, either the influence of the club propels the new member into the church, or makes him recognize that it is not "his sort," and he resigns his membership. These remarks apply to a club for games and reading, etc. Such a club should be well managed, kept scrupulously clean, well provided with games, and furnished with an excellent bar, where all kinds of cakes, nonintoxicating drinks, and tobacco can be purchased. Other clubs such as a Sick, Burial, and Annual Division Society, a Christmas Club, a Loan Club (a most useful organization), a Book Club, a Coal Club (making provision for coal at a cheap rate all through the year) should be formed and open to all parishioners. Again, a Flower Show, whether the Parish be in the Town or Country, will prove to be most popular, and in some districts a Poultry and Pigeon Show will call forth even more support. At intervals, if the condition of the district warrants it, an Exhibition of local industries will do much good. The men, through these different agencies, are helped to realize that the Church touches them at different points of their lives, and further that they are encouraged by these organizations in some

" hobby " which frequently becomes a powerful counter attraction to the public-house.

(3) *By Visitation.*—Supplementing what has been said on a previous occasion, I press for systematic visitation of men. The Committee of the Men's Service can assist in this, but the greater part of the work must be undertaken by the Clergy. I know the difficulties in the way, but efforts must be made, where it is possible, to visit in the evening, on Saturday afternoon, and, dare I add, on Sunday morning also. The last is in many ways the best time of all, for the Public-Houses are closed, men are at home and find time hanging heavily on their hands, for unaccustomed to being at home in the morning, they do not know what to do, and if a Visitor arrives with a cheery smile, he will find that a chat on the doorstep is frequently welcomed, when at another time it might be resented. The man should be touched if possible on his weak side. Some time ago, while talking to a woman on her doorstep, I caught sight of a squirrel, which I learned was a great pet of the husband whom I had long wanted to reach. Here was my opportunity. I read up " Squirrels " and then called to see the man, who at first was rather gruff, until I said " Oh, the other day I happened to see you had a squirrel, and I wondered whether I might see it at close quarters." Then I talked *Encyclopædia Britannica* on Squirrels until the man began to think I knew what I was talking about. " Squirrels " got him, and on he came to the Men's Service.

(4) *By the Study of Men.*—We must study their habits, their mode of thinking, and their life. As a medical student after studying the " Theory of Medicine " postpones the commencement of his practice until he has " walked the hospital," so the Minister should, if

possible, between his University training and his Ordination, study the class of men among whom he is going to labour, and for this purpose go into residence in some Settlement, working where the local conditions are somewhat similar to those in the Parish in which he hopes to receive his title. The Curate in Kensington will not have the same difficulties to face as his brother in Stepney, whose life again will be quite different from that of his friend in Hereford, and the wise Ordinand will study the characteristics of those who are to be his sheep. But to this subject we must refer more fully in the next lecture.

(5) *By Following Up.*—There is surely something in every man which can be said to resemble Christ, for there is "a light that lighteth every man that cometh into the world." For this "something" to be drawn out and developed, men must be followed *and* followed.

I have been asked to tell you an incident which occurred in my old parish in Holloway. I called and called upon a man whom I was most anxious to reach, but in vain. At last I determined to call every Sunday on my way to the Service, and to count the number of visits I paid before I "hooked my fish." The man got furious. Every Sunday I called, and every Sunday I was met with an oath. Time went on until one Sunday I said, "Do you know what it is to-day?" "No, d—— you, and I don't want to know." "Well," said I, "it's your Centenary." "What's that?" said he. "It means," I replied, "that this is the hundredth time I've called, and I wonder whether I shall have to make it two hundred before you come to the Service." In a fierce voice he said, almost white with passion, "D—— you, I'll come to get rid of you," and come he did ; but I never had to go after that man again. The "one hundredth call " got him, and it was worth it, for it was for such a man that the Christ shed His Blood and died. We are so easily shaken off. An agent for an Insurance Company would soon be discharged if he ceased his canvassing as easily as the Christian Visitor does. If a man swears at you, so far from that being a reason for his being left alone, it shows how greatly he is in need of the Message which you have to deliver. Persevere ! Persevere ! Persevere ! One text ought to be looked at so frequently by every Christian worker that the words " *Until* He find it " are seen over every door and upon the forehead of every man at whom we look.

Men must be reached. Posters and cards announcing the Service should be printed and found everywhere. The Church Bell is an old and valued form of advertising the commencing of a service, but another, a newer and in some respects more effective method, is that produced by the printing press. The Church cannot afford to miss it. Letters should be written to men who for some reason cannot otherwise be reached. In the street the parish priest should not walk as if aloof from men, but he should remember that all whom he meets are in his parish and as such are his sheep, and not one of them known or unknown should be permitted to pass without a friendly nod or a cheery word. Thus no charge of " standoffishness " should be possible in his case. Let him be recognized by his people as " one of themselves " in the best sense of the term ; and let him be known as one who speaks to men when they are in health and he will be the one desired when trouble or sickness appears.

(*d*) *The Object of the Service.*

(1) *Salvation.*—There can be only one object in this special work—to lead men to Christ. Nothing less will

make it worth while.   Men at heart despise the Priest of God who waters down the Gospel until there is nothing left in it but a cold and lifeless system of ethics.   Christ must be lifted up and men must be won for Christ.   St. Paul caught men wherever he went—St. Peter did likewise on the Day of Pentecost.   This, and this only, is the work which counts as real Church work, and everything else is little worth.

(2) *Fellowship, Personal Service*.—Men must be made to realize the value of Churchmanship.   The Men's Service must not become undenominational in character, or be a blind alley into which men are easily lured.   It must be a corridor through which men pass into full Church membership.   The Men's Service which does not produce Confirmees, Communicants, Church Workers, is defective and is not fulfilling the whole of its purpose.   The Men's Service is to *catch* men and when caught pass them over to the Church for the development of their Christian life.   It is in this work that so many excellent organizations fail.   They lead the soul no further, they feed it not, and then wonder that the convert, once so full of promise, has lapsed.   Recently a conductor of a large P.S.A. in London stated that out of one thousand members of his Service only thirty-three were members of his Church, and out of seven hundred members of his Women's Service only seventeen were on his roll of Communicants.   Yet there are many ways by which the Men's Service can become a feeder for the Church.   Questions bearing on the Church are sure to be asked, and they provide an opportunity for disabusing men's minds of many wrong views, which are current in workshops concerning—The Church, the Episcopate, the Connection with the State, Church Endowment, etc.

Again, the Afternoon Services can attract men to the Evening Service, if a pressing invitation be there given, and if a subject of special interest is announced. The Evening Service should be made as easy for strangers as possible. The number of the page in the Prayer Book where the Psalms are to be found should be announced. Likely men should be asked to week-day gatherings of different kinds, and so link after link should be forged in the chain which should connect the men at the Men's Service with the full life of the Church.

Thus men must be sought, and thus men can be found. It is a difficult task, and one which demands whole-hearted devotion, but it is essentially a happy sphere, for there is no joy more real or lasting than that begotten of a visit to a home happy in the love of God, where one is greeted by a wife cheerful and bright, surrounded by her children when but a few months back—that house was desolate, that wife was hopeless, those children were practically fatherless, and now this mighty change, this wonderful twentieth century miracle has been wrought by the Christ of Bethlehem and of Calvary, through the Ministry of the Men's Service. I tell you there are few joys greater than this. Thrice blessed work—Eternal work this, and it is to such work that you and I are called, unworthy as we are. Who of us, realizing the possibility, nay the certainty of such " high Calling," will permit our Ministry to aim at, or merely result in, those things which are earthly ? Let us catch men, feed men, lead men to Victory after Victory through His Name.

LECTURE THE FIFTH

In Town and Country—Differences of Operation.

A PARISH priest cannot work successfully an East End parish on West End lines, or a parish in Kensington as he would a parish in the country. There are "diversities of operations." Truth is unchangeable and eternal; methods of transmitting the Truth are as varied as are the characters to whom the One has to be presented. Each man needs Christ, and Christ alone can satisfy the hearts of men to whatever class they may belong. He is the same Christ, and the Gospel is the same Gospel in Belgravia as in Whitechapel. The West can no more do without Him and His Atoning Work than the East. But as Izaak Walton taught: "A man must be the scholar of the fish before he can be her master," and the wise "Fisher of Men" will study his people whether in Mayfair or Southwark, Marylebone or Chislehurst, village or town, before he enters upon his work and attempts to catch his "fish." Each class has its peculiarities, and its difficulties, but none are too great to be overcome in "the Name that is above every name." Let us consider in hope, and with faith, the various classes of the community to whom the Master is sending us.

I. **The Wealthy Classes.**

(a) *The Irreligious Rich.*—The wealthier classes are

fast becoming *the* problem of the Church. Speaking generally, Nonconformity has very little hold upon either the aristocracy or the extremely wealthy classes, and the Church finds her greatest difficulty in reaching men at the two extremes of society, the man of the Slum, and his brother of Belgravia, neither of whom has anything in common with the other, save the essence of his manhood and his absolute need of Christ. Among the rich there are men as faithful and as true to Christ as in any other class of society, and who hold their riches as a trust given to them by God. But alas, they are few. The West End of London is in many respects a far more difficult problem than the East End. It is the haunt of the rich men of all nations. From the Gold Fields of South Africa, from Wall Street in New York, from the great Sheep Stations of Australia men gather ; and together with the wealthy Hindoo and the continental Jew erect a strange city within a city ; and although its streets are paved with gold its atmosphere is not the atmosphere of Heaven. Here reign Luxury and Pleasure on the Throne of Materialism. Silver, as in the days of Solomon, is of no account, and a thousand pounds paid for a dinner, a hundred pounds for a jewelled collar for a favourite poodle, are squandered with a light heart simply to gratify a moment's fancy. Wealth makes the immoral life the easier, and Piccadilly has become a by-word in Europe for all that is sensual, devilish, and unclean. Yet some, while living the life of modern Sodom, will pose as philanthropists, and their gifts will swell the exchequer of the Hospital or even of the University. Such a stronghold of evil, where Satan's seat is, may appear unassailable and unconquerable, but it is not so. The Minister of God in such a city must be verily a man of

God, living as a John the Baptist, or as a Savonarola, leading in their midst a life of Spartan simplicity. This is the type of man wanted for such a post. His life, his home, his preaching must cut right across the lives of those around him. Some time ago Father Vaughan showed that he realized what was needed in the West End, but he failed largely, if not altogether, to meet the need. The preacher to such a class should be a man without regard for wealth, never bowing before it or its possessors, and never permitting men to think, even for a moment, that gifts of money can atone for sin, or that " Conscience money " can purchase an entrance into the Kingdom. The class of people which I have described are in some ways more dangerous to the State than are the Anarchists, and yet the Church seems to be unable to do anything among them. They appear to be outside her influence. The rooms and homes of the poor are visited by the clergyman ; but the drawing-rooms of the irreligious rich are frequently as far from the ministrations of the clergy as if they were on a cannibal island.

We have had Round Table Conferences on " Confession " and the " Eucharist " : surely it is time that the Round Table was called into requisition for the consideration of " How to reach the rich." I do not advise any of you to take up work among such a class unless you are specially called by God to do so, and are willing to cast aside the ease of life, and to deny yourself, taking up the Cross daily, and to proclaim it both by your life and word.

(*b*) *The Religious Rich.*—In this class we may place not only the zealous Communicant and the church-goer, but also those rich people who are not wholly given up to pleasure, and who are disposed to be friendly

to the Church and her work.   The man who works for
God among this class must be a gentleman in its truest
sense.   He must ever remember that what God wants
are the souls and hearts of men, rather than their
cheques and guineas.   The " alms and oblations " are
presented before Christ is received in the " Communion," but after His reception by faith, something
grander is offered, " Here we offer and present unto
Thee ourselves, our souls, and bodies."   The great
danger is to remain satisfied with the former.   The rich
suffer from heart-hunger even as the poor, and frequently I have been told by the rich that they sometimes wished that they lived in a poor parish, for then,
as they have said, they might receive a real pastoral
call.   There are many devoted parish priests who
minister to the spiritual needs of their rich parishioners,
but it has to be admitted that in many parishes the
rich are simply visited from a " social " standpoint.
The " call " is received, and the " call " is returned.
Something more is needed and must be given.   Some
time ago I called on a well-known peer to obtain his
signature to a Trust Deed, and was told that he was laid
up owing to trouble in his leg, but that he would see me.
After we had transacted our business, and had had a
little cheery chat, I rose to take leave.   Then it occurred to me to say—" If your lordship were a working
man in my parish, and were ill in bed when I called, I
should pray that God might bless the means made use
of for your recovery.   May I pray with you ? "   For
a moment he appeared astonished, and in rather a
stammering voice said " Yes."   I prayed, and when
I rose from my knees I found the tears trickling down
his cheeks, and he, with an English gentleman's dismay
when he finds that his feelings have overcome him, was

trying to wipe them away as he said, " Do forgive me, but I am turned seventy. I have been a Churchman all my life. I am holding many offices in the church, and I have been visited for years by the clergy, on all sorts of errands, but you are the first clergyman who has ever prayed with me, and oh ! how often have I wished some one would do so." His is not a solitary case. If tact is used, the rich are often as anxious as are people of any other class to receive spiritual help and consolation.

But opportunities have to be created. Rich men, even more than working men, are won rather by rod and line than by the net, and consequently more time has to be devoted to individual cases. For instance, could not a rich man be invited to a quiet dinner, or could not his invitation to one be accepted and then later, when alone, perhaps while smoking a cigar, the conversation could be turned into a spiritual direction. Again, Ladies' Bible Classes can be formed, and during the season of Lent or of Advent some lady might be induced to throw open her drawing-room or ball-room for a course of afternoon addresses. Some few years ago I gave a series of addresses in a house well known for its great political receptions, and numbers of people attended to whom the ordinary Lent Services held in church would not have appealed ; and better still, there were many signs of real blessing following this method of work.

The young must receive especial attention. A special gathering of Public School boys should be held every vacation. This should be of a homely, manly character, and if some clergyman who is, or has been, renowned in any part of the athletic world can be induced to give an address, so much the better. A

I

similar gathering suitable for girls away at School should be held during the vacations. Care must be taken to avoid anything savouring of cant or cheap sentimentality. The boy when at School and the youth when at the University must be remembered. A letter written to them each term will be valued, and pave the way for a closer intimacy during the vacation. A youth is very susceptible to such an influence, and a letter written to him under such conditions will make him realize that he is not forgotten. If two or three men are up at Oxford or Cambridge it will be quite worth while to spend a day off with them, having lunch with one, tea with another, and perhaps dinner with all three. This would do much to keep the clergyman in touch with his flock during the dangerous period of University life.

Although it is true that the rich enter the Kingdom of God " hardly," yet the lives of not only a Nicodemus, a Joseph of Arimathea, but many a millionaire of modern days, prove that it is possible for them to do so, and it is ours to lead others to buy the " Pearl of great price."

II. The Intellectual Classes.

The number of intellectual giants may not be so large as formerly, yet there are more well-educated people in the world to-day than in any former age. Large numbers of these have imbibed new ideas as the result of advanced scholarship, discoveries in science, greater knowledge of history and of ancient literature, and in consequence have been moved from the older presentation of various Articles of Belief, forgetting that the belief may be right, while the presentation of it may have been crude. This point of view must be realized and met. Again, as the writer of *Commerce and Chris-*

tianity says : " You have on one hand an evangelical
section, still maintaining its doctrinal fervour seemingly
by shutting its eyes and stopping its ears to all that is
advanced and authoritative in the intellect of the time ;
and at the other extremity there is a militant sacerdotal
party building up a huge fabric of learned superstition
on a basis which the sacerdotalists themselves will be
the first to declare has nothing to do with intellect or
reason, but is purely a matter of faith and of Church
Authority. In the one case, the zeal appears to the
onlooker to be the outcome of a shrinking from light
and knowledge ; in the other, it is based on a legacy
of superstition from the past." This may present an
exaggerated view of the present situation, but the
statement embodies the thought of large numbers of
the more educated classes, and this type of critic must
be met, for such an attitude of mind encourages a
religion of mere " Humanism," and such without God
sooner or later degenerates into selfishness. The
secret of the power of " Humanism " lies in the fact
that it is the offspring of the doctrine of the " Fatherhood of God," and the result of the influence, perhaps
unconsciously received, of the Christian atmosphere in
which literature, art, music has been fostered for many
generations. As a number of wagons on the railway
may pass into a siding because of the impetus given to
them by a push of the engine, although their power is
gone and they soon come to a standstill, so in the end
a detached " Humanism " will simply be stranded in a
siding and cease to be a moving power. If religion
decrease, so will the love and philanthropy of men
decrease.

Intellectual men are unattached to Christianity from
various causes :—

(*a*) *Atheism.*—Atheism is becoming less and less prominent in philosophical and scientific circles. The truth of the paradox is more realized, that only a god can prove that there is no God, and only an Omniscient and Omnipresent Being can say that no God exists. The fresh discoveries in every department of science cause the argument from Design and from the work of Nature to become stronger rather than weaker as time goes on. While, however, this is true, men are apt to be drawn into —

(*b*) *Agnosticism.*—Many admit the possibility and even the probability of the existence of a God, but deny that He is known or can be known. Such men have to be led to realize the value of the accumulative evidence of men all down the ages. St. Paul's testimony, " I *know* whom I have believed," has been the testimony of millions since his day, and it is impossible to find any fact in history, so well authenticated by the evidence of so many men of intellectual power, as is the fact of the possibility of knowing God. A man, seeing only with the naked eye, must not deny the facts concerning the stars told to him by one who has seen them through the telescope. The evidence of Newton, Herschell, or Ball, is considered by scientific men sufficient ground for the acceptance of certain scientific phenomena, and the man in the street, with such trustworthy evidence before him, does not presume to say, " It is impossible for such things to be known " ; and so the testimony of a St. Paul, a Gladstone, a Newton, a Kelvin, that they have seen the Lord, must be equally insisted upon as authoritative, and it should not be disputed by men who, from whatever cause, have not looked into the Heavens and seen Him.

Again, men decline to accept Christianity owing to—

(c) *Individual Causes*.—Some men are involved in what we may term " honest doubt," and argue that they would believe if they could. Others make a really dishonest statement as to their unbelief simply as a cover for their sin. Their sin must be denounced and their so-called doubt brushed aside, while the former class must be treated with the utmost sympathy and patience. There are also those who do not repudiate the teaching of Christianity, but they do not accept it as final or perfect, but simply as marking a stage in the development of the religious life of the world. But where do we find any ground for believing that Christianity is not final, but simply a forerunner of something higher than itself?

The Middle Ages are sometimes referred to as evidence that Christianity has failed in its Mission, but, luke-warm as the disciples of Christ have been, both in promulgating His teaching and in ordering their lives thereby, every student of history must surely acknow-ledge that the one great uplifting force in the world for the last two thousand years has been the Christian Faith. If to-day every Christian man, every Christian organization were suddenly removed from England, the contrast between the England in such a state and the England of to-day with Christianity would be simply indescribable.

Some are philosophical in their objection to Chris-tianity, although sound philosophy is more and more regarded as not only not antagonistic to religion, but as really her handmaid. On this subject it is well to read Illingworth's *Personality, Human and Divine*, and Cairn's *Fundamental Ideas of Christianity*.

Again, other men refuse to connect themselves with the Christian position, because the alleged conclusions of Science are thought to be contrary to the teaching of Holy Scripture, and also because of their difficulty in accepting the miraculous element in Christianity. Men of the latter type forget that even Huxley said : " I have not the slightest objection to offer, a priori, to all the propositions of the three Creeds. The mysteries of the Church are child's play compared with the mysteries of nature." As a matter of fact, some men permit mystery everywhere except in religion which deals with the Eternal Verities, and where from the very nature of the case mystery must prevail more extensively than in any other realm. As far back as 1833, Dr. Chalmers said in Cambridge : " Religion has nothing to fear from the advent of true Science," and no new discoveries have undermined in the slightest degree the facts of the Old Faith. It should be remembered that scarcely on any one subject has Science said its last word. It is always reopening questions, is always having to readjust its teaching, and in the opinions of many scientific authorities the gap between the Bible and Science is lessening as Science advances and the Bible is more fully understood. The miraculous is, in a sense, becoming less miraculous as fresh discoveries are made, for many of these are of such a nature that they, from their wonderful character, are greater marvels than the miraculous. Wireless Telegraphy and the powers of Radium were possible three thousand years ago, but only recently have they become known to us. So forces which are not known now to us may have caused many of the miracles of bygone days, and thus many miracles may not have been antagonistic to nature or even interruptions of the laws of nature, but actually worked in accordance with some law of nature with which we are as yet unfamiliar. Many men of Science have recognized these facts, and in such a book as *The Religious Belief of Scientists*, by the Rev. C. L. Drawbridge, we shall find that the scientific mind can also be one in which the Spirit of the Christ reigns. It is well, however, to remember that a great Scientist may be but a poor Theologian, as a Master of Physics may not necessarily be an authority on Logic. If this fact were kept in mind, it would do much to remove the adverse influence which some agnostic scientists wield, and young Christians should be warned on this matter.

The Archbishop of York recently pointed out that difficulties resulting from scientific investigation do not account for the Agnosticism of to-day, so much as do the theories about the Bible and the Atonement which are so frequently advanced from many pulpits. In connection with this subject I would recommend the reading of Rev. P. N. Waggett's book, *The Scientific Temper in Religion*.

And how are all these various intellectual difficulties to be successfully overcome ? There must be wise and careful reading and time provided for adequate thought. The standard of efficiency in the pulpit must be raised, although there are men to be remembered of the type of the great lawyer who said to F. D. Maurice concerning the sermons at Lincoln's Inn : " We have been taxing our brains to the utmost all the week, and we don't want them taxed on Sunday." But still the pulpit must be occupied by one who understands the mind of the man in the pew and who grasps his difficulties. Unless the preacher does so he is apt only to exasperate his hearers, instead of carrying them along with him. To such a congregation books and authors should be constantly recommended, for it is a lamentable fact that the vast majority of men of the professional type know little, if anything, of the great " Classics " of the Faith. How seldom are any standard works of Theology found on the shelves of, for instance, doctors or lawyers who are professedly Christian men. The ignorance on such subjects of men, who in other respects are well educated, is a great weakness which the clergy should seek to remove.

But in dealing with the intellectual classes, it is most important that essentials should be carefully distinguished from non-essentials, and that stress should be laid upon the former rather than upon the latter. Again, the circle in which essentials are enclosed should be a very circumscribed one because, when closely examined, some of what are termed essentials may in a certain sense and in certain cases be, after all, non-essentials. For example, within our circle " Belief in the Bible " and " Belief in the Church " are placed, and in a general sense both are essentials, yet what had the Bible to do with the conversion of either the Thief or the Jailer, or what had the Church to do with the former who received neither of the two Sacraments ? The Intellectual should be turned to Christ, and upon Him such men should be taught to concentrate. It is well not to argue from the circumference to Him the centre, but rather to proclaim Him. To enter into controversy concerning Him is a temptation to be resisted, for the Apostolic method was simply to proclaim Him, and He was received, not by the intellect, but by the heart with which men believed and were saved. When Christ is received, then the Bible and the Church will become essentials to men, but neither will become such until Christ has first been received. The Cross, which was to the Greeks foolishness, may appear to be the Gospel least suitable for " Intellectuals," and yet it is the one Gospel which alone can save. " Jesus and Him crucified " is, for all men, the only essential for salvation. To the man without Christ, verbal inspiration or higher criticism may becloud and perplex the intellect, but to the Christ-possessed man they are difficulties no longer, for the Spirit guides him into all truth.

Then again, both in town or country are to be found men who are not rich or poor, not highly intellectual and not among the ignorant, but are generally known as—

III. **The Middle Classes**.

The Middle Classes are designated the " Backbone of England." Men of this type are accustomed to rule, to organize, and generally " to run things," and to a large extent Nonconformity has appealed to this class more successfully than the Church. The position of Deacon in a Congregational or Baptist Chapel is one which in many respects exceeds in power and authority the position of Warden or Sidesman. In the Church the Vicar is supreme. In Nonconformity the Minister is paid by the Deacon, and although nominally called and dismissed by the vote of the whole Church, yet in practice the Diaconate of the Chapel practically determines both. It will be seen that here is found a congenial sphere for men of the middle-class type, and yet the Church can attract and retain such men. In such a parish it is most important that sermons should be good and well delivered ; that the Services should be thoroughly congregational, and well rendered ; that a Church Council with wide powers should not only be called into being, but frequently consulted, and that, as far as is compatible with our ideas of Church Order, the laity should possess real powers, and the distinctively secular part of the Church's work should be committed to their care. By means of the Sewing Meeting and District Visiting mothers and daughters should be linked with the Church, while the Debating Society and some organization like the Christian Endeavour should meet the needs of the younger generation. Some of the most successful and flourishing Churches are in middle-class districts, and there is no reason why the Church should not become the spiritual home of this important class of the community.

But the classes mentioned so far form only a minority of the nation, and the work of the clergy will largely be among—

IV. The Working Classes.

Concerning this class, Professor Peabody writes : " To the great mass of hand workers nothing would seem more unreal or more uninteresting than the ordinary methods and concerns of the Christian Church. On the day when Christians meet for prayer Trades Unionists and Socialists meet to consider what they believe the not less sacred themes of human fraternity and industrial peace." Charles Booth, after his survey of London, said : " The working classes as a whole stand outside any organized religious body." As a matter of fact, they expect nothing from the Church and they have no fear of it. When speaking on " Work amongst Men " (see page 88), I dealt with many sides of church work among the working classes and its difficulties ; but we may note a few additional points. When men are paid well, and when the hours of labour are not too prolonged, one aspect of employment is frequently overlooked. The awful monotony of various occupations seriously affects the mental and even the moral outlook. Said a man to me on one occasion : " I get to my work at 8.30 a.m. I pack a chest of tea, then another and another and another until dinner-time. Then I pack another and another until I leave off at 6.30. The next day I do the same and the next and the next, and for over twenty-five years my whole life has been spent in simply packing chests of tea." He was a thoughtful, steady man, and no one can gauge how the man's soul must at times have been seething in revolt at spending all his life, his *one life here*, in packing chests of tea. The division and subdivision of labour in recent years has tended likewise to destroy all pride which a man might have in a completed work, and has certainly tended to demoralize large numbers of working men.

Once again, the struggle for existence constantly keeps to the front the old question, " If God is love and all-powerful, why does He allow such evil to exist in the world ? " This is *the question* of all questions for large numbers of the working classes, and one which must be faced, for upon it all the rest really depends. It is this which gave Mr. Blatchford's articles in the *Clarion* any influence. Positive teaching must be given concerning the facts relating to Christianity, and the great doctrines of the Faith must be examined and evidence adduced in their support. In this connection, the following books are worthy of study : *Clarion Fallacies*, by the Rev. Frank Ballard ; Welsh's *In Relief of Doubt* ; Godet's *Defence of Faith* ; and Harrison's *Problems of Christianity and Scepticism*. In dealing with Christian Evidences I prefer the delivery of an address, with questions at the end, to a series of Conferences. At the latter the local agitator or stump orator is certain to make his appearance and to monopolize the meeting, and frequently he cannot be checked without the impression being produced that he is being unfairly treated, or that his arguments cannot be met. The working classes can be won for God and the Church by means of faith, prayer, sympathy, tact and *hard work*.

A lower class exists commonly known as—

V. The Submerged Tenth.

This is a class which excites our pity. It is the greatest blot upon our national life, and one for whose existence the State and the Church are largely to blame. Nothing except love and perseverance, coupled with sublime faith in the power of Christ " to save to the uttermost," can accomplish much among the inhabitants of the slum. Every effort must be made to alter the social conditions under which these people reside. They must be visited, visited, visited, especially when sickness makes its appearance. The Minister must be known to the Police Court Magistrate, and he must be in close touch with its Missionary, and thus every opportunity must be seized of linking himself with the real life of these people. There is much leeway to be made up, and the Church has a great task before her if this class is to be won for God. It is encouraging to hear a testimony as to the value of the work of the Church from a leading Baptist, the late Mr. W. S. Caine, M.P., who said : " As a matter of fact, the denomination that more than any other is doing the work among the poor, the miserable, the wretched, the sinful, is the Church of England." Since these words were uttered the Church Army, with its splendid record of work under Prebendary Carlile, has strengthened the position of the Church as *the* organization that is really the Church of the poor.

The child of the slum should receive the special care of the Church, for he is the offspring of conditions which have grown up largely through the apathy of the community of which the Church is the guardian. Such children must be watched over, guided in the choice of occupation, and helped to a higher life than that of their parents. In some cases emigration is the best solution of the problem of the " Slum child." Closely allied to this problem is that of the huge crowded areas like the East and South of London, and of districts of a similar nature in the cities of the North and of the Midlands. Here the Socialist finds his goods for the shop window which he exhibits to the world as evidence of the evil results of our present industrial system. It is not my province to discuss the economic questions connected with Socialism ; but, as a non-Socialist, I protest most strongly against the practice, so common in many quarters, of linking Socialism and infidelity together. That there are Socialists who are infidels, is as true as is the fact that there are Liberals and Conservatives who are atheistic in their opinions. It is equally correct that some socialistic advocates, both by pen and speech, teach infidelity ; but it is quite as unjust to take such to be the real leaders of Socialism as it would be to take a Mormon as a concrete example of Christianity and its teaching. Some of the finest types of Christians in the East End are Socialists, and one regrets that by confounding Socialism with Anti-Christianity the work of the Church is frequently made more difficult.

By the side of the slum-dweller lives the Alien. The problem of the alien is great, but it has been grossly exaggerated. The number of aliens in this country is less per cent. of the population than that of almost any country in Europe. The real difficulty connected with this problem is caused by the congregation of a large proportion of the alien population within the circumscribed area of Stepney, Whitechapel and Spitalfields. Yet it must be remembered that as a whole the aliens, contrary to popular belief, form a law-abiding community. In 1910 the total acts of crime by aliens of every sort in Great Britain and Ireland numbered 2,271, and of these twenty-five per cent. were committed by Americans. The Jews do not drink ; they are thrifty, and are exceedingly fond of their children. Infantile mortality among them is some forty per cent. less than it is among their Gentile neighbours. Whatever view the politician may take of Alien Immigration, it is clearly the duty of the Church to succour and to help those who come among us. Even under the Old Dispensation, the Jew was exhorted to love and help the stranger in his midst as though he were " Home-born." By the Incarnation and the Atonement these men are revealed to us as " brethren," and our duty to them is manifested all through the teaching of our Lord. The worker who would succeed amongst this class must learn their language, study their habits, accustom himself to their mode of thought, and must be untiring in zeal and devotion. There is scarcely any task more difficult than that which is to be found within a few miles of St. Paul's Cathedral, where, in street after street, not a single English home is to be seen. Special men are needed for this special work, which, in many respects, has been largely neglected. Few men consider its claims, which in some ways are as great as are those of China or India, and a still smaller number volunteer to devote their lives to the solution of the problem which it presents.

Again, the Church has to realize the great difference which exists between the work in a town and that in a country parish.

VI. In Town and Country.

In a town the parish priest is tempted to become a mere machine, one concerning whom it might almost be said that he had solved the secret of perpetual motion ; while in the country, the danger lies rather in the small incentive which a village gives to the Minister as an encouragement for him to be at his best personally and for him to do his best work. In the country the population as a rule is so small that the Pastor has no great difficulty (except in extremely scattered populations) in knowing all his sheep by name, whereas in the town parish of ten or even twenty thousand this is impossible. In the one there are numbers to cheer, while in the other the lack of numbers tends to depress. The Minister in the one parish lives in the midst of activity and excitement ; the Minister in the other parish is apt to chafe at the monotony of his life and work. Yet, whether in town or country, the difficulties are no more, rather are they immeasurably less than those which were overcome in the early days of Christianity. Let us consider these different spheres and in the first instance endeavour to realize—

(a) *The Importance of the Country Parish.*—The clergyman in the country district must not despise his high calling and his great opportunity. His influence may be greater and more permanent than that of his brother in the town. If the Church and all for which it stands were removed from the rural life of England, then England would be poor indeed. The history of both Church and State reveals the fact that the greatest sons of each, the men who have really made England great, have been the children of the village rather than of the town. Again, in recent years the city life of England has been largely influenced by the influx from the village.   The exodus from his parish makes the work of the village clergyman all the more difficult, but here lies his opportunity.   Can he send forth men of God into the towns, men who will not be captured by the glitter and pleasure of city life, but will tend to purify and elevate it ?   From a small village during one year forty-five young men recently passed into the towns. If young men could come forth clean and strong to battle for the right, then the cities of our land would be strengthened by their advent.   But what of—

(b) *The Difficulties of the Country Parish ?*—Villages differ as towns differ.   The old village dating back to the days of the Normans is not exactly similar to the village which came into being but yesterday, simply because of the railway which runs through it.   Each has its own peculiarities, and each has much in common with its neighbours.   The isolation and the monotony are to be found in both.   The tendency for the clergy to degenerate mentally and spiritually, requires the utmost vigilance and the closest walk with God if it is to be overcome.   A congregation of about twenty, of whom perhaps six only will be men, is apt to tempt the preacher to look upon the sermon as something which requires no great preparation.   If only his work lay in town, then, he is tempted to think, it would pay to prepare ; but here it is a mere waste of time, unless the Squire will be at home, and with his guests will attend church on the Sunday morning !   Such a line of argument is fatal to the spiritual life, not only of the village, but also of the Incumbent himself.   No man can continue doing work inferior to that of which he is capable without himself becoming inferior in consequence.   The Minister must give of his best, always and everywhere, not only because of the call of duty, but for his own sake and in defence of the maintenance and increase of his own spiritual life.   In his parish of five hundred all his sheep must be known by name.   They are all his flock.   He is specially sent to them.   That old man who can only talk " pigs," that wife whose main concern is the care of her chickens, that awkward lad who knows little but the plough—all of these are immortals, and the immortal can never be commonplace.

The motto of Bishop Hackett is one for every village rectory : " Serve God and keep cheerful."   The village Pastor may find the visit to the Squire congenial and useful, but his main work will lie with the villagers. He must enter into their life and order his own the better to meet theirs.   If the all too brief hours that the labourer can call his own clash with the Rectory dinner-hour, then the mid-day meal must be sub- stituted for the dinner at the later hour.   The true Pastor will be the centre of the recreation of the village, and of the little club and entertainment in the winter. Knowing as he will the temptation which the town pre- sents to the young of his flock, he will endeavour to counteract it by increasing their love of the country and its life.   He will realize that one cause of the desertion of the village is the lack of eyes to see its beauty, and the village lad and girl will be taught to see by the road-side, in the field, and among the trees, the wonders and marvels of vegetable, animal and bird life.   The young people, especially after Confirmation, will be given some little work for God.   It may be by joining the Choir, or by taking a small class in the Sunday School.   The preparation of a suitable Cantata or Service of Song would cheer the winter evenings.   The village Orchestra, so ruthlessly and unnecessarily expelled from our churches years ago, could be re-

K

introduced, and thus fresh interest would be aroused, not only in the Church Services, but also in the life of the people themselves.

The wise Pastor will preserve the mornings for reading, and as far as his means permit he will always have at least one new book upon his study table. Ian Maclaren's *Days of Auld Lang Syne* and *Beside the Bonnie Brier Bush* will give him courage to face his work manfully and with hope. Yet he will remember that the vocabulary of the villager is exceedingly limited even in this twentieth century, and that even in English it is possible to violate the Article which decrees that our Services must be in a language understandable by the people.

The Blessed Master loved the village and His disciples were sent through those of the Holy Land. It was from the lily, the birds of the air and the harvest-field that lessons were drawn which men are learning to this day, and happy is that Pastor who finds in his village a sphere blessed of God.

I pass now to another branch of our general subject—

VII. **Special Kinds of Work**.

During recent years a great change has been effected with regard to parochial activities. Formerly, beyond the Services on Sunday and on one week-night little was expected in the parish, excepting a Sunday School and perhaps a Band of Hope. Now, agencies have been multiplied and each section of a parish expects separate and distinct treatment. Work among men has already received attention, and we must now consider—

(a) *Work among Women*.—The change in the position of women in recent years has not been altogether free from grievous disadvantages. The hurry and bustle of city life, together with the abandonment of the quiet of the home, has acted detrimentally on the nervous system of women, and has seriously contributed to that hysteria which is manifesting itself, on the one side in the methods of the Militant Suffragettes, and on the other in the appalling and apparently uncontrollable drinking habits of thousands of women. At one Metropolitan Police Court, out of 151 persons committed to an Inebriates' Home only 28 were men; while at another, out of 138 persons so committed only 15 were men. At the Police Court of one of the great cities of the North, the following figures afford sufficient evidence as to the terrible increase of drinking among women. Out of persons convicted—five times for being drunk, 1,067 were men, 1,671 were women; ten times, for every 1 man there were 3 women; twenty times, for every 1 man there were 6 women; thirty times, there were only 4 men to 70 women; forty times, there were only 1 man to 32 women; fifty times, there were no men to 14 women. In the North of England, and to some extent in the Midlands, gambling has greatly increased among women, and even female "Bookmakers" are now quite common. These facts emphasize the great importance of steady work among women at the present time. The ordinary Mothers' Meeting does good, and yet the spirit underlying the reply of a woman who had been asked to attend one is still alive. "What! Me come? I'm hard up, but I've not come to *that* yet." The utmost care should be taken lest women come for what they can get. Addresses of a bright, homely, straight, Gospel nature should be given, interspersed occasionally by one dealing with some aspect of Domestic Economy.

The Mothers' Union is an excellent institution, and

lays particular stress upon the sanctity of marriage and the importance of the home. The weakness of the usual work amongst women, which confines itself to Mothers' Meetings, Unions and Services, lies in the fact that numbers of women are unmarried, or, if married, have no children, and such as these have no place in the Mothers' Gatherings. In my own parish at Bethnal Green we started some years ago a special Service for *all* women. It is held in church every Monday night at 8 o'clock summer and winter alike. Mothers are not encouraged to bring their children, as it is generally understood in the parish that Monday night is the women's night *out* and the men's night *in*, and that the father must watch over his children one night a week. The Service largely corresponds to the Men's Service, excepting that the Orchestra is composed entirely of ladies. The address at this Service must be very simple, and the preacher cannot adopt either the style or the matter of a Men's Service address. He must be bright, remembering the sombre lives of many present, and must have a message of hope and cheer. The Service for women is now a recognized and valued adjunct of the Church's work.

There is also room in the parish for a Church of England Women's Society with practically the same rules as the C.E.M.S. Such a Society can materially help the work of the Church. The sick can be visited by its members, and during the week following the Administration of Holy Baptism a member can call at the home of the child and leave the Baptismal Card, and also have a talk with the mother on her responsibility to God and the child. Other members can collect the Missionary Boxes once a quarter, open them, count the money, and affix fresh labels to them. The

Rule of Life deals with the duty of Prayer and of Work, and the advantage of the C.E.W.S. over the Mothers' Union is that it is more comprehensive, and that it can unite more easily the keen women of the parish to further the different branches of the Church's work.

(b) *Work among Young Women.*—In the wealthy parish and among the educated classes stress should be laid upon the obligation of service. The modern Women's Movement has not received that guidance from the Church which its importance demanded. Yet the Church can provide a far more legitimate and useful sphere of service for women than the State. The Women's Settlements and College Missions have rendered excellent help in many districts ; but in many other directions educated women can be found a sphere of useful service. The Teaching profession, for instance, in a poor district, affords opportunities so great that they can scarcely be exaggerated. The " Happy Evenings " on week-days, a Saturday afternoon Ramble, a Bible Class on the Sunday, can all be utilized by the Teacher in addition to the influence which a good woman can wield all through the week on child-life.

The girl in the middle-class parish is, as a rule, fairly well educated, and is generally the kind of girl who, if wisely guided, can be kept in touch with her Church. In some districts, as the Bishop of Edinburgh lately pointed out, the Young Women's Christian Association provides just the kind of comradeship and work which such a girl desires ; but in parishes where, for various reasons, this Association does not exist, then a Young Women's Guild or Club should be formed. The rules should be few, and the latitude given fairly wide. The Bible Class should be its centre, but the Club must be attractive, the refreshment bar dainty, and the programme varied. A musical evening once a week, a Sewing Class for the poor or for the sale of work, a St. John's Ambulance Lecture, a Cookery Class, and a night in the Gymnasium : these are a few ways in which the week's programme can be filled.

The Girls' Friendly Society is most useful, and its rules and methods of work should be carefully studied. The efforts of this Society to befriend girls as they move from one part of the country to another are excellent, and deserve all the assistance which the clergy can give to them.

The Factory Girl, such as is found in the East End of London, presents a difficult problem, but one worth solving, and one which can be solved. She is the product of the uncivilized mode of life which has been allowed to develop in our great cities during the last fifty years. She is sent out to work at the earliest possible moment among girls of her own class who, in the aggregate, are usually " game " for anything. Her home is so overcrowded that, as more babies arrive, she is practically told to go and make room for them, and is forced into an early marriage, which is so disastrous an element in the social life of the worst districts. Yet this girl when reached frequently becomes " out and out " for God and the Church. Boisterous and rough, and " tom-boy," as she often is, she possesses traits of character which, if only drawn out and developed, make her a splendid soldier of Christ. The Club for this class must not be too palatial, for if so the girls will not feel at home within it. The Conductor must be a real leader, possessed of tact and of boundless sympathy. Most of all, the religious atmosphere must be maintained. The closing hymn and Prayer, night by night, are most important, for the homes of many girls are such as to make it impossible for any private devotions. The Bible Class must be kept well to the fore, for, by themselves, the civilizing influences of a Club are, after all, little use to such a girl in the midst of the appalling temptations which surround her. Therefore it is essential that Christ should be proclaimed in a simple, homely and reverent way, and that the girls should be led straight to Him.

In the North of England a very different type of girl is found in the weaving-shed. She earns good wages, and the methods advocated above must be modified in many ways if she is to be won and retained for the Church.

Again, the girl fallen from her purity must be treated no more harshly than the man who is the cause of her trouble. She must be treated as her sister was treated by Christ. This class of work must be largely done by women, but must always have the sympathetic and prayerful assistance of the clergy.

(c) *Work among Young Men.*—This work requires a manly man or a really womanly woman for its head. In some few cases I have known most successful Young Men's Bible Classes to be conducted by a lady, but generally this is a type of work best done by a man. Whether among young men of the status of the clerk, or of the more refined artisan type, or of the rougher coster or porter class, the Bible Class must be the centre of any movement for influencing them if it is to succeed. The first step must be to create a large Bible Class. The net used must be a big one. Young men wherever they are must be button-holed, at the church doors, in the streets, on the football field ; and the Conductor and his Committee must be always on the watch for recruits. Cards announcing the Class and giving information concerning the Club should always be carried and ready for distribution. The room in which the Bible Class is held is an important factor in making it a success. It must be bright and cheerful, for if it has a cold, bare appearance, and if the seats are uncomfortable, the light bad, the heating apparatus out of order, and the piano or harmonium out of tune, the Bible Class will soon become a thing of the past.

The Class to be really aggressive should consist of young fellows of a very varied type. The keen Christian, who is anxious to work for God, comes to the Class for help ; the half-hearted Christian, the backslider, the careless, and the indifferent—all these ought to be reached and held together in the Class. This was done with excellent results in two Bible Classes conducted by former curates of mine, the Reverends George Twentyman and E. A. Dunn. The lads composing them were of a somewhat different social grade, and yet both were eminently successful. One plan was to divide the time of the Class into two parts, the first part consisting entirely of hymn-singing. In some Bible Classes an Orchestra of the members could be formed to accompany the singing. The Class proper should commence with Prayer, the members standing meanwhile. The notices and a hymn would then follow. The lesson or address should avoid those pitfalls which Mr. A. C. Benson so graphically describes in his *Upton Letters*, and no vivid death-bed scenes should be recounted, but on the other hand a religion full of life should be presented, for it is life and not death which appeals to young men. It is not always advisable to " read round," for even in these days reading is sometimes a difficulty.

A Gospel or " The Acts of the Apostles " can be

taken as the subject for the winter and dealt with verse
by verse. Now and again a change can be made by
holding a " Question Sunday " which is most useful.
Purity or Temperance will be sure to arise in the Book
selected, and then the whole afternoon can be spent
on these important questions. The lads wear a badge,
and have a registered number which they give as they
enter the Class, and so absentees are known and regu-
larly visited. The " Inner Circle " of Communicants
are set to do work either in the Sunday School or in
the Open Air, and for such they are carefully trained.
A Foreign Mission Band helps materially to increase
the sums contributed for Our Own Missionary. Part
of one of the large galleries in the church is reserved
exclusively for the members of the Young Men's Bible
Class, and it is no uncommon sight to see fifty or sixty
young fellows present at Morning Prayer, and double
that number in the evening. Although weekly Communion is strongly advised, a Corporate Communion
once a month is arranged, and a preparation class is
held on the Friday previous. Every opportunity is
utilized for strengthening the spiritual side of the work.
A Conference on Good Friday from 5 p.m. to 11 p.m.
has become an annual fixture, and is conducted by the
fellows themselves. From this Bible Class several
Candidates for Holy Orders have been obtained, and
assisted through their training. Several members are
at present labouring in various parts of the great
Foreign Mission Field.

The Club side of the work must be well arranged.
The rules should be few. The age limit should be, say
from fifteen to twenty-one years. The Vicar should
act as the Warden, and should appoint the sub-warden,
who should be the Curate in charge of the Club. It

is well to have inserted in the rules a proviso that all alterations are subject to the approval of the Vicar and must be countersigned by him. The Committee should be elected partly by the members and partly by the Warden. In addition to such games as Chess, Draughts, Dominoes, and Bagatelle, Billiards may safely be introduced provided that the game is paid for *before* being played. Cards in a Young Men's Club should be strictly prohibited. Smoking must be permitted if the Club is really to capture young men from the street, but an age limit of eighteen years should be fixed and no smoking allowed under that age. The refreshment bar should receive special attention and be made attractive. The outdoor games of cricket, football, tennis, hockey and swimming (in the Public Baths) should be encouraged in every way, for it is only by such means that the tendency to imagine that "Sport" simply means watching others play a game can be checked. In the winter a "Parliament" can be elected and a Government can be overthrown and a patriotic Opposition installed in its place.

The Bible Class and Club must be looked upon in its Mission character. Its aim must be to bring to the Church a rich Harvest. Classes should be formed at least three months previous to Confirmation and the subject should be dealt with on the Sunday previous to the commencement of the classes. Emphasis should be laid on the fact that attendance at these classes does not necessarily involve Confirmation. The spiritual tone of both Bible Class and Club must be maintained or both will fail ; but if faith, prayer and effort combined with common sense are the watchwords of the Warden and his Committee fruit is certain, and fruit worth possessing, for it will be eternal in its duration. The principles which govern Young Men's Bible Class and Club work are the same whether for the artisan or the rougher type ; but the above methods should be altered and adapted to meet the requirements of different localities.

Work among young men and women can be influenced very largely by—

(*d*) *Work among Children.*—For many years work among children has been placed in the forefront of the Church's work, and both in the Day and Sunday Schools she has given of her best to child-life. It is, however, to be feared that the relative increase of efficiency in the religious training of children has not kept pace with the improved methods of modern secular instruction. It is therefore incumbent upon the parochial clergy to seize every opportunity of coming into touch with child-life. If a Church Day School is in the parish, and if it is part of his duty to give religious instruction, the wise clergyman will prepare his lessons most carefully, realizing that even when at his very best his lesson is likely to compare to his disadvantage with that given by the trained teacher of the school. If he can arrange to take a course of instruction in methods of teaching, which is now frequently available in different centres, under the auspices of either the Church of England Sunday School Institute or some similar body, he will find that in many ways his teaching is likely to become not only much more interesting, but also far more effective. The clergy should seek to make it clear that they do not desire to supersede the Day School Teacher, but simply to supplement his teaching. We must now consider various methods of work among children.

(1) *The Sunday School.*—In modern days the Sun-

day School has been, more than any other agency, the centre of the Church's effort to train the child for God and for the Church. With all their limitations Sunday Schools have done much for England. When it is remembered that it is entirely a voluntary system, the result of no legal enactment, and with no official attendance officers whipping up the children, the attendance of millions at these schools Sunday by Sunday is really marvellous, and compares most favourably with that of the Day School. The devotion of the vast army of men and women, young and old, who, year after year, give their Sundays to this work, affords one of the grandest examples of self-denying Christian work in connection with the Church to-day. It is well that the parish priest should remember this fact when apt to criticize the results of Sunday School work, and to comment adversely upon the quality of the teaching given and upon the illiterate kind of teacher which is sometimes found in his Schools. The religious life of the country would be the poorer, and that in no slight degree, if Sunday School work ceased to exist. The Sunday School must be made as efficient as possible, and the first effort in this direction should be to improve the status of the teacher. Men like Lord Hatherly, Earl Cairns and Earl Selborne continued their Sunday School work while holding the position of Lord Chancellor, and the co-operation of men and women of education as teachers should be secured if it is at all possible. The Teachers' Preparation Class should receive careful attention, and the Model Lesson, given by the clergyman, should be for children of a medium age, and the teachers should be shown how it can be extended to suit older children, and also adapted for the younger. For the average teacher I recommend one of the Oxford

Bibles with its mass of information as a help to the study of the Bible, *Cruden's Concordance*, Thompson's *Land and the Book*, Geikie's *Hours with the Bible*, together with a book on *Sunday School Teaching* by the Rev. H. A. Lester, and for Junior teachers *New Methods for Juniors* by Miss Hetty Lee. The Preparation Class should not be fixed for the latter half of the week, for teachers are apt to leave all preparation until after it has been held. The best day is Monday, because then the teacher will have the whole week to think over the suggestions made.

Two methods of teaching may here be mentioned : (*a*) *The Marden Method*, which divides the School into three grades following to some extent the Standards in the Day School. In each of the three grades several classes are taught all the same lesson, and the children are not moved up for two years. (*b*) *The system known as that of St. Sulpice*, and originally used by the Roman Church for teaching the Catechism in Paris, and which was made known in England largely through the writings of Mr. Spencer Jones. The system is most elaborate and one which in many respects is not easily adaptable to English Church life, even the Roman Church in England, as Bishop Gore points out, finding it difficult to introduce.

Whatever efforts are made to increase the efficiency of the School, its main object must always be kept in view, and that is to bring the children to Christ. In levelling up the educational side there is a danger of secularizing the sacred character of the work, so that the Bible is simply taught in the Sunday School as History is taught in the Day School. Sunday School lessons must consist both of teaching and of exhortation. All undue emotionalism must be discountenanced, but, on the other hand, it must be recognized that children of the tenderest age can and do give their hearts to God. The " Except ye become as little children " of our Lord shows that children possess just the faculties which enable them to enter the Kingdom. This, then, must be the aim of all Sunday School work, and although lessons on the Old Testament have their place in the Syllabus of Sunday School teaching, the fife of our Lord (as described, for instance, in Dr. Eugene Stock's admirable lessons) should ever hold first place. The Catechism must also be taught if our children are not to grow up without the Church setting of Bible truth. The neglect of the Catechism, and the indifferent and uninteresting teaching frequently given upon it, is a distinct loss not only to the child, but also to its Churchmanship when an adult ; and clergy especially are responsible for seeing that this department of Sunday School work is done efficiently. Occasionally teachers object to teaching the Catechism on the ground that they prefer to give Biblical teaching. This difficulty can only be overcome by the teachers themselves being taught that Catechism teaching is nothing but the *very essence* of New Testament teaching, and that it can be made at once interesting, instructive and spiritual. The upper classes in a Sunday School should use the Catechism with a view to Confirmation.

(2) *Children's Services.*—Sponsors are enjoined to call upon children " to hear sermons." Sometimes this injunction is used as an argument that children were meant to be present at the Holy Communion, because in that Service provision is made for a sermon ; but a similar provision is made in the Marriage Service and no one would consider that an appropriate service for children. It is often expedient that Services for chil-

dren should be entirely separate from the ordinary
Church Services.   In this way the conduct of the Service and the nature of the address can be made far more
suitable for children than is possible in a mixed congregation.   This Service should not be held on Sunday
afternoon, because that would be destructive of the
Sunday School, and also because that is the best time
for the Men's Service, whereas Sunday morning and
evening is the best time for children.   In a very poor
parish it is well that children should be taken out of
the street, and even out of their homes, as much as
possible on Sundays.   This necessitates the Services
being held in a hall, but this can easily be given an
aspect differing from that which it bears on the week-
day at school or at the Band of Hope.   The table may
be covered with a cloth and flowers placed upon it, or
in some other way the difference may be emphasized.
Thus the Day and the Service are marked off from week-
days and their usual engagements.   The Conductor,
who may be a layman, should arrange the programme
and invite speakers, but it should be a rule that occasionally the address should be given by one of the
Clergy, who in this way will be kept in touch with the
Service.   It is advisable that separate Conductors be
appointed for the Morning and Evening Services so
that they can attend the ordinary Church Services once
each Sunday.   At this Service the Prayer Book can be
used in a modified form, and the children will thus get
accustomed to it.   The interest of the children can be
encouraged by one of the elder boys reading the Lesson
(the Scripture Union portion for the day), and by one
of the girls singing a hymn or solo.   The address can
be founded on the Epistle, Gospel, or one of the Lessons
for the Day.   The majority of the children will be

found at the Children's Service, but some will always be found with their parents in church, and for these a Children's Hymn should always be provided at Morning Prayer and occasionally a " Five Minutes' Talk " to them should precede the Sermon. Of course, united family worship in the family pew is the ideal, and in some classes of society this condition may prevail to such an extent as to make a separate Service unnecessary. Sir William Robertson Nicoll has lately founded among Nonconformists a " League of Worshipping Children," having for its object the strengthening of the ties which bind the child to the Church, and its methods are well worthy of study. Such a spirit must be fostered to the full, but unfortunately in the majority of cases no family religion is known, and it is for children in such a position that the separate Service is mainly intended.

One word on the question of Sunday School prizes. The fact that there are dangers connected with their distribution should not cause their discontinuance. Scholarships and Exhibitions are freely given in other walks of life, and the carrying off of a Sunday School prize is a great event in the lives of many children, and the books thus obtained are frequently held as a treasured possession even in late life.

(3) *Children's Guild.*—In former days the most popular week-night gathering for children was the Band of Hope, and undoubtedly the present position of the Temperance Movement is largely due to former work among the children. To-day, however, a somewhat broader view is advisable, and a Children's Guild is more calculated to cover the ground. If this is formed, then the subjects can be varied from week to week. The first week can be devoted to Temper-

ance, the second to Foreign Missionary stories, the third to games, and the fourth to the Scripture Union, and where a fifth night is available in the month to " Kindness to Animals." The Lantern can be used occasionally (not too frequently) with advantage. If the Guild is to be successful the leader must be bright and hearty, a good disciplinarian, and a real children's friend.

Other important adjuncts of Children's work are—

(4) *The Church Lads' Brigade*, which is excellent when well organized. Its Bible Class, together with the discipline of the military training, have been most beneficial in many districts, and rendered good service to boys at an age when they are most difficult to retain.

(5) *The Boy Scouts' Movement* has captured in a few years the imagination of the boy life of the nation as no movement has ever done before. How lovable is the boy of the large town, keen, alert, full of mischief and fun ! What is not worth doing or giving to help such a boy as I think the Bishop of London describes ? Here is one, selling evening papers and yelling lustily, " All the winners, All the winners," when he sees coming in his direction a stiff and proper clergyman, for whom such a cry would have no attraction. Immediately he is equal to the situation and the street echoes with his call " Terrible fire in Jerusalem ! " This is the type of boy which the Scout Movement catches, licks into shape, and turns out as a good citizen and a manly man. The Scout Promise reveals its strength.

1. " I will be loyal to God, and the King."

2. " I will do my best to help others whatever it costs me."

3. " I know the Scout law, and will obey it."

L

It may be well to note the following :—

(*a*) The value of the Scout Movement is that it makes an appeal to the imagination of the lad of spirit, and directs his oft-misguided energies into right channels.

(*b*) The troublesome boy who gets into scrapes must not easily be thrown outside, for he is the one who frequently turns out a splendid fellow.

(*c*) When the troop becomes large, with forty or fifty or more boys enrolled, it may be well to hand it over to some qualified layman who will act as Scoutmaster, but in doing so the clergyman should neither retire from the work nor become merely the Chaplain.

(*d*) When a troop reaches forty in number an additional Scoutmaster can be appointed, and therefore the clergyman should still retain that rank, as this position in the troop will give him a valuable hold upon the lads.

(*e*) The boys should be divided into two divisions, those under fourteen and therefore are still at school, and the lads over fourteen who are at work.

(*f*) If possible, during the summer, the troop should be taken twice a month at least into a forest for a march, or into the country for a paper-chase or for Scout games. A summer camp is likely to be most helpful, but frequent week-end camps are not recommended as they tend to slackness on the Sunday.

(*g*) The Bible Class should be kept well in front, and all that we as Churchmen desire for our boys can be obtained through connection with Baden-Powell's Movement.

(6) The Girl Guides, under Miss Baden-Powell's directions, are doing a similar work among girls. The principles are the same as the Scouts, but the methods

employed are, of course, different, and the subjects taught more varied.

Whatever methods are used among boys or girls, they should be of such a nature as to form a connecting link with the Young Men's or Young Women's Guilds, and thus form the bridge over a dangerous period of school age and youth.

The essential qualification without which no work among children can ever be successful, is love to children. Given that, and even workers of inferior intellectual gifts will do much excellent work, Some few years ago, Bishop Creighton visited the celebrated Children's Home situated in my parish, founded by Dr. Stephenson, an ex-President of the Wesleyan Conference. As the Bishop and the Doctor were going the round of the homes, a number of the children rushed to the Doctor's side, pulling at his coat tails, holding on to his arms and hands. The Bishop (knowing how frequently in such Institutions things are prepared for a distinguished visitor) turned to me and said : " That cannot be organized. Children cannot be made to do that to order." This was very true, and if a clergyman gives himself to children, their loyalty and their love are assured, and he can do more than " Suffer the children," he can bring them himself to the Lover of Children, their Saviour.

Thus we bring our consideration of the variety of operations necessary to reach different classes of the community to a close. No class of society is easy to reach, for sin is found everywhere, but each class can be reached, for the Saviour is not the God of the rich, or of the poor, but of all men.

Washington left a home of refinement to become the father of his country : Lincoln, lowly of origin and deficient in education, saved his country in its hour of need : Shaftesbury, from the home of aristocracy, became the friend of the miner and the factory hand : Livingstone, from the tiny cottage, became immortal as a Discoverer and a Missionary. The city of God can be entered from the North, the South, the East and the West : so we can gather the eternal fruits of our Ministry from the rich, the poor, the learned, the ignorant, for God is the Father of all, and Heaven is prepared as the Home for all. It is in reliance on the Fatherhood of God, the efficacy of the Saviour's life and death, and the call by the Holy Spirit, that we go forth to all men proclaiming the Gospel of Christ, knowing it to be the power of God unto Salvation to every one that believeth.

LECTURE THE SIXTH

In Building up the Church

A N army to be successful must be efficient, and efficiency is not obtained without thought, pains, and effort. As with an army, so is it with the Church, although her weapons are not carnal but spiritual. On the day of the Ascension the Church was not sent immediately into action, but into retirement. The command, "Go, hide thyself," always precedes the order, "Go, show thyself." The Church must always tarry until she receives the "power," but, when once that is obtained, the gates of hell shall not prevail against her. Thus equipped, even in Jerusalem, peopled with men who slew her Lord, she gained a victory, and thousands were made captives in His Name.

The first step in preparation for the Church's Battle is, as it ever was, to ascend into the Upper Room, and this leads me to consider the value of united Prayer.

I. **The Prayer Meeting.**—The Prayer Meeting has been maligned. It has been called a Nonconformist Institution and a Salvation Army method, and its Apostolic origin has been forgotten, yet in the Upper Room the Church was born in its midst. The Rev. C. Harris (a Priest Associate of the Confraternity of the Blessed Sacrament) says : " The only religious movement of recent times which has excluded Prayer Meetings is the Oxford Movement. The attitude of the High Church Party as a whole towards Prayer Meetings is to be regretted, because it deprives them of one of the most potent means yet devised of Evangelizing the masses and kindling enthusiasm." In the last few years, largely owing to the influence of the C.E.M.S., Prayer Meetings have been commenced in many parishes where hitherto they had been under a ban. The chief objections to these gatherings are the length of some of the prayers and the irreverent expressions which are occasionally used. That in extempore prayer there is a danger of things being said which "jar" upon our ideas of reverence is only too true, and yet it should be remembered that language which might be utterly out of place in a drawing-room in Belgravia, may in Whitechapel be quite harmless. Bishop Creighton once spoke to me on the question of applause in church during an address, and his advice was, "Do not encourage it," but do not unduly frown upon it, for, at St. Paul's, Onslow Square, they say Amen, at St. Alban's they sing "Stainer's" Sevenfold Amen, and in a third case they may say it with a stamp, and who is to say which is really the most reverent of the three, but He Who sees the heart from which the sound comes." Can we not say the same concerning some of the expressions heard in a Prayer Meeting? They may appear to us to be irreverent, but are we sure that He to Whom they are addressed regards them as such? Still careful and kindly teaching of reverence in prayer and praise will do much to keep the Prayer Meeting on right lines. It is equally true that older men may tire and weary people with the undue length of their petitions, but a private request to these to shorten their intercessions for the sake of younger and less experienced people usually will have the desired effect. The Prayer Meeting should be commenced punctually, suitable hymns should be sung, and a short address given. The subjects for prayer should be selected before the meeting commences, and as each is mentioned, silence should be observed for a space, and then an extemporary prayer offered. The last five minutes might be utilized for an impromptu litany, the conductor saying, for instance,—" That it may please Thee to bless those persons who have been recently confirmed," and the response following, " We beseech Thee to hear us, Good Lord," and so on, until various petitions have thus been offered. Hints as to the conduct of such Prayer Meetings will be found in *The Churchman's Prayer Manual* by Canon Bullock-Webster, and a pamphlet issued by the C.E.M.S. written by the Rev. C. Harris on the *Conduct of Devotional Meetings* will also be useful.

The Daily Services should become real Services of Intercession. If such gatherings are given a foremost place in the work of the parish, it will have a considerable influence on the habits of prayer among the people, which is all-important. Can we doubt that it was the five hours spent daily in prayer and meditation which has given Bishop Andrewes his influence in the Church to-day and for all time, and therefore, in the building up and consolidating the work of the Church, we give to prayer and intercession a foremost place. We pass to something equally important.

II. **Bible Study.**

Recently Canon Scott Holland said : " If you would be good Catholics, you must be Bible Christians," and he was right. The least spiritual, the least aggressive periods of the Church's history are those when the

Bible was least known and least read. But the Bible must be taught, if its beauties are to be seen, and if it is to become the " Thus saith the Lord " to men and women. The Bible Study Class Lesson must be carefully prepared, and the conductor must give of his very best. Here he must be the teacher and treat " big " subjects. My plan, which has greatly increased the interest in the Bible in my parish, is to draw up in September of each year a list of some fifty subjects. These are printed and sent to all communicants asking them to vote for twenty-five (one for each Wednesday until Easter). The list is made up of a variety of subjects—such as " the Bible and Missionary Effort," " Christ and Social Problems," " The New Testament and the Doctrines of our Church," " Difficult Texts," " Contradictions of the Bible," and the teaching of different Books. The voting is very keen, for upon it depends our programme for the winter. Persons attending the class are asked to bring a Bible and a Prayer Book, and to come prepared to take notes. The class is opened with hymn and prayer. The first five minutes are spent in answering any questions bearing on the previous week's lesson. Then usually I speak for an hour. Then follow questions (not discussions) for half an hour, and this is frequently all too short for the purpose. Another excellent method is to make a thorough study of one book the entire work of the class for the Winter. This is the plan adopted by Dr. Campbell Morgan, of Westminster, whose methods of Bible Study are so well known. A class of this nature will assist men to see the beauties of God's Word, will create and foster a taste for it, will show a man how to dig for its treasures, and how to make use of them when found. It is not sufficient that the Bible should merely impart knowledge. Men must be taught how to use the Bible as our Lord used it in the daily battle of life. One reason why so few people really love to read the Bible is because it has never been to them a book to which they have been taught to turn for comfort, for guidance and for strength for the daily conflict. The Church which has learned the secret of prayer, and has realized that the Bible is the Sword of the Spirit, is the one prepared for action and for victory. With the Bible in her hands the Church learns that power can be obtained for her baptized children by prayer, and the " laying on of hands." This brings us to another means of grace.

III. **Confirmation**.

It is not our province to trace the history of this Rite, or the varied conditions under which it has been administered. In our own Church, it is generally recognized that the period of preparation is of the utmost importance, not only to the candidate, but also to the Church herself. As Canon Newbolt so well says, " Confirmation candidates are not simply to be drilled in class, but are individual souls to be saved." If this were realized more widely the leakage after Confirmation would be largely reduced. The Prayer Book states that children should be confirmed " when they come to years of discretion." This has been variously interpreted, but I am strongly of opinion that, excepting in very special cases, it is not advisable to confirm candidates under fourteen. The argument is adduced that it is better to confirm before the girl or boy goes out to work, and much may be said in favour of such a course ; but in actual practice, it is found that instead of Confirmation helping the boy over the period in which he exchanges school for business, the reverse is frequently the case, and the change of life, startling in its novelty and bringing in its train a certain amount of independence begotten of earning money, simply puts Confirmation in the background. The boy who has gone "through" Confirmation and has not realized its benefits, is apt to throw everything overboard. Whereas, if Confirmation is deferred, and the boy kept in touch with the Church and handled lightly and wisely, he will probably begin to realize that in the world he will have to fight, and this is the time for the clergyman to step in. Lads of sixteen to eighteen have in my experience stood far better than those confirmed at an earlier age. Of course there are some girls and boys of twelve or thirteen who are quite as suitable for Confirmation as those of riper years, but they are exceptional cases. It is perhaps well to utter a word of warning against the practice of insisting, or even suggesting, that all choir boys should be confirmed. Over and over again I have known boys who were confirmed under such conditions, who, the moment their voices "broke," left the Church, for really they had only a kind of professional interest in the rite.

The period before Confirmation should be utilized for instruction and preparation. The latter is the more important of the two, but the instruction must be as thorough and as comprehensive as possible. The great doctrines of our faith must be taught, and there should be put before the candidates clearly but fully a conception of Churchmanship, which will enable them to realize, to some extent, wherein they agree, and wherein they differ, from Christians in other religious bodies. The failure in this respect is largely responsible for the tendency of many in later life to wander about, saying that one denomination is as good as another and so on, for the Church to them simply differs from other places of worship because in it a liturgy is used. The historical continuity of the Church, its comprehensive and distinctive teaching, its threefold Ministry, and all that this involves of reverence, order, and the linking up with past ages, all this means little or nothing to the Churchman whose instruction previous to Confirmation has been scrappy and defective. The preparation should not be hurried, and at least ten classes should, if possible, be held.

Important as the classes are, even more so are the private interviews with the clergy. It is advisable that they should number two at least, the first at an early stage of the preparation, and the second just previous to Confirmation. They should be homely, friendly, and to the young, fatherly, and of such a nature that through life the candidate will not so much look at the minister as a priest, but rather as a man of God, full of the Spirit of Christ, tender, sympathetic, wise, one to whom he can turn with complete confidence in any hour of need. The personal and spiritual touch will do far more than any official idea to cause the candidate in after life to regard the clergy as the priests of God and of the Church. The purpose of the interview must be to press definitely for decision for Christ and the acceptance by faith of Christ as the Saviour from sin. Although the candidate's vow, " I do," has a place, and that an important one, in the service, it must never obscure the primary object of the service, which is the confirming, the strengthening of the candidate by God Himself, by the gift of the Holy Spirit. If the cases mentioned in the Acts are used in support of the Church's practice of the " laying on of hands," it must be remembered that in them nothing is said of the vow or promise of the candidate, but the statement is always made that following prayer and the laying on of hands a gift and blessing were received. The Confirmation Service is drawn up in this spirit, and the prayers of the Bishop, the first more general, and the second distinctly special and individual, show that the candidate is expected to prepare and look forward to the day of Confirmation as a Pentecost, a day when he receives the " power " which will confirm his faith and strengthen him in the battle of life. To put the vow in the first place is to court failure, for the moment it is broken the candidate is apt to be discouraged, and to think that his Confirmation has been in vain. It is well to call the candidates together on the night previous to the service, for the purpose of explaining it to them, and also of intercession on its behalf.

The Confirmation itself must be followed by every possible effort to keep in touch with the candidates. Instruction must be given regarding Holy Communion, and at least one private interview should be obtained during the first year. An annual reunion of all con-firmees does much to keep candidates in touch with their Church, and for this purpose they should be pressed to forward changes of address, even when far away from the parish. The invitation to the reunion provides the Vicar with an opportunity for writing a letter to each candidate. I have had testimony from communicants in Australia, Canada, and all over the world as to how greatly these are appreciated. One point more. The Archbishop of York frequently asserts that Confirmation is the Layman's Ordination for Service. This should never be overlooked, and candidates should, as soon as possible, have some suitable work found for them, and thus be taught that they are not made members of the Church merely to receive, but to give, not merely to be ministered unto, but to minister. Work for God promotes unity, and strengthens faith, and makes more real the connection with the Church which Confirmation involves.

IV. The Place of Confession.

That Communicants, and especially those young in years, desire and need the help of their parish priest is recognized by every Christian worker, and for such spiritual help provision is made in the Prayer Book, and communicants are exhorted to come to the minister and—

" *Open their Grief.*" This subject has been the cause of much controversy. On the one hand, it is urged that confession as understood in the Roman Church is here enjoined, while, on the other hand, any attempt to carry out, even in the simplest form, this direction, has been viewed with suspicion as tending to reintroduce the " confessional " into our Church life. It is not our province to attempt to discuss the advantages or disadvantages of " confession " as generally understood, but we may note—

(*a*) That whatever the words in the Exhortation may mean, they do not relate to the normal, but rather to the abnormal condition of the life of the communicant. He is to quiet his own conscience if possible by certain methods clearly laid down for his guidance, and it is only when he finds this impossible, that he is enjoined to come to the minister of God's Holy Word to open his grief. Ordinarily he is to prepare his own heart for the reception of the Holy Sacrament, but a means of help is provided for him, in special circumstances, when his own efforts fail to bring him peace.

(*b*) That the compilers of the Prayer Book evidently

intended to effect some change concerning this particular question. This is apparent to any one who compares the Roman Missal, the First Prayer Book of Edward VI, and our own Prayer Book of to-day. The words altered, substituted, and omitted, are numerous, important, and strikingly significant. Some of these may be noted : " Let him open his grief " takes the place of " confess " and " secretly " ; " That the Ministry of God's Holy Word " is substituted for " That of us, as of the Ministers of God, and of His Church " ; the words " and the same form of Absolution shall be used in all private Confessions " are entirely omitted ; the Sentences, General Confession, Absolution have been introduced into Morning and Evening Prayer, together with the Decalogue and Kyrie into the " Communion Office " ; the caution " against offence with those who still practise secret confession " is omitted ; the proposal to substitute in the Exhortation the word " Priest " for " Minister " was defeated in Convocation in 1662. The total effect of the accumulation of these and other changes is very great, for in *every alteration* made the tendency was without exception against the practices of auricular confession, as it was generally understood at that time. Some change was evidently intended, and the Homily on " Repentance " reveals what was in the mind of the Reformers. " I do not say," so runs the Homily, " but that if any do find themselves troubled in conscience, they may repair to their learned curate, or pastor, or to some godly, learned man, and show the trouble and doubt of conscience to them, that they may receive at their hand the comfortable salve of God's Word : but it is against the true Christian liberty, that any man should be bound to the numbering of his sins, as it hath been heretofore in the time of blindness and ignorance."

(c) That the " benefit of absolution" was to be received by " the Ministry of God's Holy Word." The changes made in Morning and Evening Prayer and in the Communion Service help us to understand what is intended by these words. The " Sentences" of God's Holy Word which precede the General Confession and Absolution are the ground of our hope. " If we confess our sins, He is faithful and just to forgive us our sins, and to cleanse us from all unrighteousness. " Wherefore I pray and beseech you to accompany me with a pure heart," because " He pardoneth and absolveth all them that truly repent," and so, " let us beseech Him to grant us true repentance, and His Holy Spirit." In the Communion Office, the connection between God's Holy Word, the Confession and the Absolution is equally clear, but the procedure is reversed. After the Confession and Absolution, the trembling soul, who may still be half doubtful, is reassured, as he is exhorted to " Hear what comfortable words our Saviour Jesus Christ saith unto all that truly turn to Him," and also to learn from the mouths of two witnesses, of no less authority than St. Paul and St. John, how he can obtain forgiveness and be at peace, for he has " an Advocate with the Father, Jesus Christ the Righteous, Who is the Propitiation for our sins." There can be no doubt that in the public services that the " benefit" of absolution (as distinct from the Absolution itself), which is a " quiet" conscience, is intended to be secured by " God's Holy Word." If a man is still restless and uncertain, it is to the priest who, in the language of the Prayer Book, is called " the discreet and learned Minister of God's Word," that he is to repair, and to him he is to " open his grief" : that by the " Ministry of God's

Holy Word" (the same means, be it noted, as are adopted in the Public Prayer) he " may receive the benefit of absolution, together with ghostly counsel and advice, to the quieting of his conscience, and avoiding of all scruple and doubtfulness."

We see, therefore, that the priest must labour to be a " discreet and learned Minister of God's Word." He must know it through and through, so that no matter what his parishioners' trouble may be, he may know (as our Lord did in the Temptation) where to lay his hand on that particular " salve of God's Word " applicable to the trouble. He will thus know how to use " the Keys of the Kingdom of Heaven," which are, said Chrysostom, " the knowledge of the Scriptures," while Tertullian called them " the interpretation of the law," and Eusebius " The Word of God." His commission, " Whosoever sins ye remit," (which, it should be remembered, was only inserted in the Ordinal in the latter half of the fourteenth century) should, as Jewel points out, be linked to his further commission, " Be thou a faithful dispenser of the Word of God," and his private " dispensing the Word of God " will all tend to increase confidence in the " Comfortable Words," and to enable men to " quiet " their own conscience in Public Prayer in the manner prescribed for their guidance in the Prayer Book.

In many parishes no facilities are afforded by which burdened souls can obtain that help which individually they have a right to receive. The dread of being " a suspect " has frequently deterred clergy from announcing any set hours when they can be seen by those who seek comfort. It cannot be too strongly emphasized that the Prayer Book does take serious notice of the demand of the soul when in trouble, to receive assurance, and frequent opportunities ought to be provided for the ministry of it to men through the Word. In many parishes the Church is a far more suitable place for such interviews than is the Vicarage, but wherever the place, the opportunity ought to be provided, as directed by the Prayer Book. In my own ministry private and individual dealing with burdened souls has been of the greatest possible use, and any minister who discards it, is not only neglecting a most important part of the work entrusted to his care, but also is in danger of failing to gather some of that rich and spiritual fruit, which is only found, when a Nicodemus finds his way into our presence, it may be, in the solitude of our Church.

V. Fasting.

Fasting is not merely a Roman practice. It is something more. It was both taught and practised by our Lord, and therefore the Church has always regarded it as a means of grace to be used by all Christian people. The wise pastor will endeavour to present the true ideal of fasting to his flock as it was understood in the New Testament and practised in the Primitive Church. The Church of England clearly calls upon her members to fast, but leaves them entirely unfettered as to the method by which the rule is to be observed. It may be well therefore to point out :

1st. That in the Primitive Church Fasting meant much more than mere abstinence from food. The Fathers realized that in both the old and the New Testament the Saints as well as their Lord abstained from both food and drink for certain periods, and that their example was one to be followed, but they taught that fasting meant much more than this. Quotations as to their teaching might easily be multiplied, but the following may be said fairly to represent the teaching of the

M

Primitive Church on the subject. St. Gregory the Great writes : " Fasting consists not merely in strict abstinence from lawful food, but in entire separation from sinful practices, and in the hearty doing of right things. If thou seest an enemy, be reconciled to him ; if thou seest a poor man, take pity on him ; if thou seest a neighbour prospering, thank God for him." St. Basil said : " The true fast is estrangement from evil." This aspect of fasting should never be overlooked. To dwell unduly on abstinence from food will tend to lower the ideal of a true fast and to limit the benefits to be derived from it.

2nd. That the Church of England lays down no rules as to the methods by which the Fasts enjoined for Wednesdays, Fridays or the Lenten periods are to be observed. The substitution of fish for meat at these seasons may be a fast to some, while to others it may be an agreeable change rather than an act of self-denial, and therefore the Church demands no observance of this or any other custom. Her members are left entirely free to choose as to *how* they will keep the Fast.

3rd. That the Church of England nowhere enjoins the compulsory reception of the Holy Communion while fasting. In 1893 the Upper House of Convocation for Canterbury passed the following resolutions on the subject.

" That at the Reformation the Church of England, in accordance with the principle of liberty then laid down, ceased to require the Communion to be received fasting, though the practice was observed by many as a reverent and ancient custom, and as such is commended by several of her eminent Writers and Divines down to the present time."

" That regard being had to the practice of the Apostolic Church in this matter, to teach that it is a sin to communicate otherwise than fasting is contrary to the teaching and spirit of the Church of England."

The Bishop of Chester in his recently issued book entitled *Anglican Pronouncements* deals fully with this question, and clearly shows that the resolutions to which I have just referred embody the teaching of practically the whole Church since the Reformation. Therefore if a person finds that by coming fasting to the Holy Communion he is helped to obtain a greater spiritual conception of Christ, he should be advised so to communicate, but on the other hand the teaching of compulsory Fasting Communion can have no place in a Church which uses in its prayer of Consecration the words, "*After* supper He took the Cup." The Church lays down no rule on this question either in the list of "Fasts" or elsewhere. Each communicant is left entirely free to follow that practice which he finds most beneficial to the building up of the Spiritual life. While, however, avoiding these somewhat side issues, the parish priest will do well to teach clearly the duty of fasting in its full meaning of self-denial. The age is rapidly becoming tainted with softness, luxury, and the abandonment of any restraint, and it is therefore most important that the Church should teach moderation in, and for certain periods abstinence from, food, together with any other restraint which may tend to bring the body into subjection. Fasting in some way or another is an essential of the Christian life, and as such must be taught and encouraged.

VI. The Holy Communion.

"Feed My sheep" was one of the last commands of our Lord. There are many ways by which the sheep can be fed, but in the Holy Communion we possess one which was ordained by Christ Himself. What is meant when we utter the words " Feed upon Him in your hearts by faith with thanksgiving " ? Is Christ really received by faith ? If in this service He is verily and indeed received by the faithful, then the clergy should (to quote the rubric in the Office for the Communion of the Sick) exhort them "particularly to the often receiving of the Body and Blood of our Lord Jesus Christ when it shall be publicly administered in the Church." It is sometimes erroneously stated that the rule of the Church is, that the confirmed should communicate three times in the year, but the provision for the administration of the Holy Communion every Sunday throughout the year, in addition to the celebrations on Saints' Days, surely emphasizes the desire of the Church as to the " often " receiving of this Sacrament as enjoined in the Rubric. The experience of many clergy reveals the fact that many come but once after Confirmation, while others content themselves by merely communicating at Easter. If the Church life is to be sound, vigorous, and spiritual, the Holy Communion must occupy a very prominent position in the life of its members. The Preparation Service on the Saturday night is helpful, and the use of suitable hand-books is also beneficial, but it should not be forgotten that at the first Celebration those communicating did not previously know that there was to be one, and our own Prayer Book Service is so arranged that the Service itself can be made into a very real preparation. The value of this Sacrament for the building up of the spiritual life must be distinctly taught, and every opportunity which the Church authorizes should be freely afforded by the clergy, while the laity should be instructed as to the value of frequently participating in this Holy Sacrament.

VII. Service in Soul Winning.

The Church is to be fed.   Fed in the Prayer Meeting, in Confirmation, through the Ministry of God's Holy Word, by Fasting, in the Holy Communion ; the Church is thus to become strong, but strong for service.   She is to tarry and hide herself that she may be ready when the command is issued " Go," " Show thyself."   The Motto of the Salvation Army, " Saved to Serve," has been the motto of the Church militant from the beginning.   Gibbon tells us that in the earliest days of the Church her members realized that " it became the most sacred duty of a convert to diffuse among his friends the inestimable blessings which he had received." They remembered not merely the command, " Take eat," but also the *last* command of all, " Go."   They realized that the command was not merely meant to be obeyed by the Church in its corporate capacity, but that each man, each woman, was personally commissioned, and " they went everywhere preaching the word."

The priest, ordained to seek for scattered sheep, will rally to his side all members of his Church.   He will teach them that they were received into the Congregation at Baptism not that they might be merely fed and nourished, and become the recipients of heavenly gifts, but rather that they might carry out in their lives the object which the Church had in view, when she received them into her midst.   " We receive this person into the congregation of Christ's flock, and do sign him with the sign of the Cross in token that hereafter he shall not be ashamed to confess the Faith of Christ crucified and manfully to fight under His banner against sin, the world, and the devil ; and to continue Christ's faithful soldier and servant unto his life's end."

His attention will be called to the words, " to confess the faith," " to fight manfully," " to continue Christ's faithful soldier and servant." He will be shown that the obligation of the new member of the Church Militant is here set forth. No easy path is presented before him. No allurements in the form of blessings are held before his eyes. He is to be a soldier, to fight and win souls for Christ. The failure on the part of so many to perform the task thus set is largely due to the Clergy who do not emphasize in their teaching that it is more blessed to give than to receive from the Church. No Church can be strong until this is realized. Each man and each woman must be out to win souls. The words of two great preachers of the last century may well be quoted : Spurgeon said : " If the Kingdom is ever to come to Our Lord, it never will come through a few ministers, missioners, or evangelists preaching the Gospel. It must come through every one of you, in the shop and by the fireside, when walking abroad and sitting in the home. You must all of you endeavour to save some one." Henry Ward Beecher was equally emphatic in the same way : " The longer I live the more I value those sermons where one man is the Minister, and one man is the Congregation ; where there can be no doubt as to who is meant when the Preacher says, " Thou art the man."

Thus by individual dealing, by direct testimony for Christ, the members of a Church must gather into the fold the erring and the lost. The spirit of the Brotherhood of St. Andrew must be that of the whole Church. Instances of the fruit of individual work must be brought forward. It was an old woman that brought Bunyan to Christ. Wesley was not converted by means of a sermon, but by conversations with a Moravian.   The lives of St. Francis of Assisi, St. Catharine of Sienna, and Archbishop Fénelon reveal how their best work was done when dealing with individual souls.

The value of one soul should be proclaimed until each member of the Church realizes his responsibility to God for the salvation of those around them.   Mr. J. R. Mott states that if every Christian brought one person to Christ each year, the whole world would be converted in twenty-five years.   " How to win souls " should form the subject of many sermons, and men and women should be shown how they can watch for openings, and by conversations, the distribution of tracts (wisely selected), the ministry of song, definite and persistent prayer for individuals, and in other ways seek to win men for Christ.   The winning of souls for Christ will do much to strengthen the faith, to promote the unity of the Church, and to bring her members themselves very near to their Lord.

VIII.   The Place and Work of C.E.M.S.

The growth of the C.E.M.S. has been phenomenal. It is safe to say that it is unique in the history of the whole Church.

Never before have one hundred and twenty thousand communicants, all men, been banded together for so distinctly spiritual an object.   It knows nothing of party politics, and has within its ranks Liberals, Conservatives, Labour men, and Socialists, " All in One." Party divisions in an ecclesiastical sense count for nothing.   The C.E.M.S. knows nothing of such. Neither is this a society for working men nor for Dukes. It recognizes no class distinctions, but seeks to bind Churchmen of all classes, of all schools of thought, of every variety of political colour, in one united body for one common object.

The condition of membership is very simple, and yet very comprehensive. A member must be a communicant. The Society rests upon that for which the Holy Communion stands, the Broken Body, the Shed Blood of Jesus Christ her Lord. The badge is the empty Cross on which the Body was broken and the Blood was shed. The rule of life leads the member Godward and manward. It emphasizes the need of constantly using the road to God, which was opened out by the Broken Body and the Shed Blood, and thus prayer becomes the rule of life. But as men look into the face of the Father they see it turned in the direction of men for whom the Body was broken and the Blood shed, and so they turn manward to " do something " for the Church in order that men may be won back to God. It will clearly be seen that the whole conception is spiritual. The Society is intended for spiritually-minded men, bound together on a spiritual basis for a distinctly spiritual object, to be achieved by distinctly spiritual methods. The Society's work is not merely to conduct debates, or to arrange for Dances or Whist Drives. Its task is far higher than that. It is to do something to help forward the Church in its great task of making all men the disciples of Christ. The first step in the accomplishment of the work is to induce every communicant to become a man of prayer, and a man of work. The Branch will arrange for its Prayer Meeting, its corporate Communions, its Bible Study, and in every way to seek to make its members strong for service. It will also arrange for them to take their part in Visitation, in Open Air work, in Missionary efforts, in Social Service, and in Morality campaigns. Members will be taught their financial obligations to the Church. They will be encouraged to read books on the history, doctrine, and work of the

Church at home and abroad. Their enthusiasm will be aroused through the reading of the lives of her saints and warriors.

Care must be taken lest it should be thought that all work must be initiated, organized, and carried through by a Committee. Men should be taught to be original and to find work for themselves. The clergy must not hold aloof from the movement, for it is not a laymen's society. No *Church* society should exclude the parish priest, and the Society's Motto, "All in one," is meant to bind clergy and laity together more closely for united service. The Minister will therefore do well to foster every phase of work undertaken by the Society as a whole, or by its members as individuals. He will make known, for instance, such an act of Moody's, who, on his conversion, sought in vain for Christian work at the hands of the Church with which he was connected, took and paid for, even though occupying only a poorly paid post at a draper's, two pews, and these he filled Sunday by Sunday with young men whom he induced to attend. Everything should be done to return to the idea of the Primitive Church that every communicant is meant to be a worker, and every worker is expected to be a communicant. The C.E.M.S., whether worked as a Branch or as a Federation, must keep this ideal before it, and if it does so, then it will prove itself to be one of the most powerful factors in the spiritual life of the Church and of the nation.

IX. A Broader Outlook.

If the Church is to be strong, and if it is to fulfil its purpose, it must never become congregational or parochial in its outlook and work. Belief in the "Holy Catholic Church" and prayer for "the *whole* state of Christ's Church militant here on earth" must not only be expressed by the lips, but by the whole attitude of the mind and work of each member of the congregation. He will look beyond the boundaries of his parish and its church, and will realize his oneness with all Christian people throughout the world. He will realize that loyalty to his own Church is compatible with co-operation on many subjects with those outside her ranks. In England, Nonconformity is of two kinds, that of the Romanist and that of the members of what are generally known as " The Free Churches." Both had their origin in the Church of England, and both have for very different reasons left her. The Romans refused to follow the Church in her repudiation of the supremacy of the Pope, and of many non-Catholic accretions of the Roman system, and may be said to have finally left the Church and formed themselves into a separate body in the sixteenth century. As the Archbishop of Canterbury recently pointed out, it is probable that, notwithstanding the increase in the number of priests and of buildings, the Roman Communion is making very little headway in this country. The percentage of marriages performed by her priests has actually decreased in recent years. In 1866 they were 48 per thousand, while in 1909 they had dropped to 42 per thousand. When it is remembered that the Roman Church insists most strongly on the marriage of her members being solemnized by her priests, these figures are most striking and suggestive.

The Free Churches, in recent years, have reported a serious decrease in membership. It is well to remember that the cause for the large number of different sects in England is not so much due to the Church as to Nonconformity itself. The number of splits and divisions among Nonconformists far exceeds in number the direct secessions from the Church herself.

On such questions as Temperance, Purity, and Gambling, Churchmen should co-operate with men of every religious belief. The fact that the Bishop of London and the Rev. F. B. Meyer have been able to co-operate in such work, has been of inestimable benefit to the cause of morality in London, and the parish priest should seek to follow this notable example, and strive to unite in his parish all Christian people on a common platform when such questions arise. But beyond the Social lies the Spiritual, and it is little use to pray that " our unhappy divisions " may cease, unless we make efforts to cause them to cease. Too great speed in this direction is apt to retard rather than to advance this object. But the holding of united open-air gatherings on a Christian Evidence platform, or meetings for united prayer at the beginning of the year, cannot but be beneficial, and can be held without any sacrifice of principle on either side. In some districts the clergy and Nonconformist ministers meet for the purpose of the mutual study and discussion of the great doctrines of the Faith. This is all to the good, for although the day has not arrived for organic unity even to be attempted, yet all Christian people should strive to promote that unity by mutual goodwill, prayer and effort.

It must be recognized, however, that although Churchmen should express their sympathy with every effort which tends to promote " religion in their country, yet as Churchmen their main thought and chief effort must be directed to strengthen the work of their own Church. It is difficult to understand the position of a Churchman who would contribute large sums to an undenominational hall, and would leave the Church near by with inadequate buildings and staff. It therefore behoves clergy to cultivate among their congregations the broader rather than the parochial outlook, and to join as far as possible in all united efforts of the Church in the deanery, the diocese, and the nation.

(a) *In The Deanery.*—The clergy should themselves set an example by attendance at Ruri-Decanal Chapters, and by friendly association with the clergy of the neighbouring parishes. The work of the C.E.M.S. through its Federation can form another connecting link with the Churches in a district. United Open-Air meetings and processions in the Summer, and gatherings on behalf of Foreign and Home Missions in the Winter, are some of the means by which concerted action can be secured with great advantage to both parish and deanery.

(b) *In The Diocese.*—Work which it is impossible for individual parishes to undertake, can frequently be performed by the Diocese as a whole. Diocesan Funds are now raised for such objects as the training of candidates for Holy Orders, the supply of additional clerical and lay workers, the building of churches and halls. These should be supported by the whole Church. It is believed that when the new Finance Scheme is at work, the Diocesan Conferences will more and more assume, not merely the responsibility of raising the funds necessary for such work, but that they will become the controlling voice in their distribution, and therefore it is well that clergy should clearly lay before their people their obligation to take part in these matters which affect the welfare of the Church as a whole.

(c) *In the Nation.*—The position which the Church

occupies in the Country gives her not only an unique opportunity, but an overwhelming responsibility. Her connection with the State and what is known as her " Establishment " are frequently misunderstood. When England's first King sat on his throne in 800 and her first Parliament met in 1265, she was already established as the Church of the land, and both King and Parliament recognized the fact. The State pays neither her bishops nor her clergy, and last year she raised nearly eight millions of pounds for the prosecution of her various activities, thus showing that she does not rely solely upon her endowments for her work.

The recognition by the State of the position of the Church, and in a certain sense her partnership with her, increases the Church's obligation to discharge to the full the duties which her high position entails. That the Church is endeavouring to fulfil her obligations is admitted on all hands. In the poorest districts she is found continuing her beneficent work when frequently other Christian activities have ceased owing to the poverty of the neighbourhood. In the East End of London it is not organizations such as the Salvation Army which cover the field, but the old Church who sends her clergy, her nurses, her women workers into every slum, and it is to her clergy and the " lady " from the Church that the slum-dweller turns in his hour of need. The Church differs from every other religious organization in the Country inasmuch as she can never withdraw and leave any district without her ministrations. Other bodies may and do withdraw owing to the increased poverty of the people, but the Church must remain. The Church may be the Church of the rich, she may not be mainly that of the middle classes, she may not have captured the great mass of the working classes, but she is essentially the Church to which the poor turn, and turn not merely for the loaves and fishes, but for sympathy in their heartache and comfort in their sorrow.

But how much remains to be accomplished before England is won for God! The social conditions under which tens of thousands are living must be altered, and to this work the Church must devote herself. As Frederic Harrison says, " Economic Science has done its best and its worst with social problems, and now moral teachers must step in." Here is the Church's opportunity. It is not her province to say how the thing is to be done. She is not to embody her views in a Bill to lay before Parliament. That is the work of statesmen; but the Church must labour and labour until she has aroused the consciences of men, so that no matter what the political party is, to which they belong, they will rise and demand that in some way " slumland " shall be made to cease, the wealth begotten of labour shall be more equally distributed, the rights of men to sufficient hours of leisure for the increase of their physical, mental and spiritual powers shall be fully recognized and the morality of men shall be made easier, not merely by legislation concerning Intemperance, Impurity and Gambling, but by the efficient administration of such laws when passed.

That he may be a more efficient leader in all these great movements the parish priest should make himself conversant with the Economic questions of the day. He should understand the inwardness of the Land Question, of Poor Law Reform, of the present-day conditions of Labour and the problem of the Unemployed and the Unemployable. But he must not by these studies be drawn aside from his real work. The man lying at the gate Beautiful did not receive alms, but he found a friend who, in the Name of Christ, did that for him which no one else could do. This is in reality the work of the minister. In the Name of his Lord, he is to do for England what Parliament and statesmen cannot do. He is to proclaim through Christ a full Salvation. For this purpose all Home Mission work, such as that accomplished through such well-known agencies as the Church Army, the Church Pastoral-Aid Society, the Additional Curates Society, will enlist his sympathy and that of his people. His Church will realize that she is part of the Catholic Church in this Country and will gladly contribute her full share of workers and money for the maintenance of her work for God in the nation.

(d) *In the Colonies.*—In recent years England has been exhorted to think imperially. It is not our province to determine whether there was any justification for this veiled rebuke of the Nation for its supposed neglect of the Colonies, but it is certain that the Church has not a clean record in this respect. In almost every instance she permitted her sons and daughters to cross the seas, to settle in their new homes, without making any provision for their spiritual needs. Cape Colony was conquered in 1806, but no missionary was sent there until eleven years afterwards, and no bishop for forty-one years. Canada was under our flag in 1713, but no real effort was made by the Church until 1787. Australia had to wait until 1836 for its first bishop. The Church is suffering to-day owing to her [neglect in the early days of what we must now term " sister nations," for colonies they have ceased to be.

The need for vigorous Church life in Canada, Australia and New Zealand is very great and urgent. The difficulties are not slight ones owing to the immense distances, the overwhelming size of both dioceses and parishes and the shortage of men. Efforts to meet the need are being made by the Colonial and Continental Church Society and the Society for the Propagation of the Gospel. Recently the Archbishops' Western Canadian Fund and the British Columbia Church Aid Society have undertaken work in Canada, but there is equal need and equal opportunity in Australia and in other parts of the Empire. Whatever the Church at Home may do on behalf of Foreign Missions, she must never forget her responsibility for her own kith and kin across the water. If the lives of Selwyn, Patterson and Hannington and the publications of the Societies mentioned above were more read, English Churchpeople would understand the importance of the work which they are called upon to do, and would be the more keen in their discharge of it. Every emigrant from our parishes affords an opportunity for bringing the needs of the Colonies before our people.

(e) *In the World.*—The Church is meant to be the Church Universal. The declaration of God's love was to the World through the Saviour of the World." The command given to the Church was " Go into all the world." Here she has her marching orders. The Church militant must fight in every clime and with men of every race. The Lambeth Encyclical of 1897 recognizes that this is " the primary work of the Church, the work for which the Church was commissioned by the Lord," and the Archbishop of Canterbury says, " that among all the duties and privileges of the Church the place of Foreign Missions must occupy the central place of all."

The last century has been one of marked increase in

Missionary enthusiasm and work, but the Church has to confess that she has not by her Faith overcome the World. The millions of China, India and Japan have yet to know Him as the " Life of the World." The British and Foreign Bible Society, has in over one *hundred years* circulated some two hundred and twenty million portions of Holy Scripture, but the population of the world to-day is sixteen hundred millions. Last year it circulated seven million copies, but in the same period thirty-eight million Chinese passed away from earth. These facts are only two among many which might be adduced to show how slowly the work proceeds and how totally inadequate to the needs of the world are the efforts which the Church is making to-day.

Yet the world was never so accessible to the Missionary as now. By railway, steamer, and even aeroplane, the world from the point of accessibility is growing smaller year by year. The door is open everywhere, and from everywhere comes the cry, " Come over and help us." Bishop Hartzell writes : " Yesterday Africa was the continent of history, of mystery, and of trading. To-day it is the continent of opportunity." The Bishop of Madras says: " Give me the men and I can see my way for the baptism of ten millions of people during the next ten years." It is to this call that the Church at home must respond, not merely for the sake of the heathen, but also for its own preservation and progress. In this connection Bishop Selwyn's well-known words may be quoted : " It seems to be an indisputable fact that however inadequate a Church may be to its own internal wants, it must on no account suspend its Missionary duties ; the circulation of its life-blood would lose its vital power if it never flowed forth to its extremities, but curdled at the heart." The Church

which is not keen for the world is not found to be keen
for the slum in its midst. It is the duty of the minister to stimulate by every means in his power the interest and enthusiasm of his people in Foreign Missions.

But this can only be begotten by prayer. It was
after the descent of the Holy Ghost in the Upper Room
that men laid their lands and money at the feet of the
Apostles. It is equally true that not until after that
Prayer Meeting did the Apostles proclaim Christ to
both Jew and Gentile. The old method is the one
method for to-day. " Prayer does things," says S. D.
Gordon—and the more a parish gives itself to prayer
for Missions the more it will give of money, the more
men and women will go forth from its midst as Mes-
sengers of the Glad Tidings.

But to sum up. If the parish is to be keen about the
slum in its midst ; if it is to take its part well and
faithfully in the work of the Church in the deanery, in
the diocese, in the Nation, in the Colonies, nay throughout the whole world, the minister must lead the way.
The officer is the first to advance in the rush upon
the enemy's camp, and the minister's command must
never be " Go," but " Come." He must be in the
forefront of the battle. He must lead in prayer, in self-
denial, and in work. None of his comrades should ever
be allowed to get in front. He must be first in holiness
of life, in love of men, and in devotion to his Lord.
His Lord died for men, and he too will gladly lay down
his life for men.

May I, in my closing words, appeal to you, my
younger brethren. My own life and ministry are
largely in the past. Yours, if God wills, are in the
future. What a joy it has been to be called of Him, to
be engaged in His Service. Never a sacrifice but always

an honour to be counted worthy to fight in the midst
of a district like the East End. But, looking at my
ministry, I feel as Coleridge did when he said, " So little
done, the vast undone." The ones reached, the thousands not touched ! We think of our successes, but
God knows of our failures. They seem to loom larger
and larger before our eyes as the sun begins to go down.
What a ministry it *might* have been !   What trophies
might have been won for God but for the lack of faith
and the loss of power ! Nothing now can atone for the
failure of the past. He only can forgive, but the more
His mercy, His forgiveness, and His love are realized
and claimed, the more sorrow fills my heart that He
should have received such poor service at my hands.

You are looking forward not backward. I beseech you
to give Him all your life. Make it as full as you can.
Make it, by close communion with Him, like unto His
own life. Lose your life for His sake and you will
surely find it. " The Son of Man came not to be
ministered unto, but to minister," and the sons of men
who would be honoured with the gracious title of
" minister " must, as they live, daily " lay down their
lives for the brethren "—

> " Measure thy life by loss instead of gain,
>   Not by the wine drunk, but by the wine poured forth,
>   For love's strength standeth in love's sacrifice,
>   And whoso suffers most hath most to give." [1]

In Christ and His immortal sacrifice alone will be
found the inspiration for all this—Ecce Homo ! Be-
hold Him, till you are compelled with the intensity of
your whole being to cry—

> " Love so amazing, so divine,
>   Demands my soul, my life, my all."

[1] " The Disciples," by Mrs. H. E. Hamilton King.

A sermon, a ministry, a life so inspired, so full of the Master Himself, cannot fail to present to men the irresistible appeal of divine love. " In weariness and painfulness, in watchings often, in perils in the city," and feeling " daily the care of all the Church," but strengthened and maintained by Christ the Living Bread, you shall bring a fruitful ministry to a glorious close, and humbly say with the warrior apostle, " I have fought a good fight, I have finished my course, I have kept the faith."

Printed by BUTLER & TANNER, *Frome and London*